To David,

Happy Christmas 1992.

NATURAL WONDERS
OF THE WORLD

NATURAL WONDERS
OF THE WORLD

JOYCE ROBINS

HAMLYN

Half-title: Iguaçu Falls, Argentina

Title page: El Capitan and the Yosemite Valley, California, USA

Published by
Octopus Illustrated Publishing
part of Reed International Books Limited
Michelin House, 81 Fulham Road
London SW3 6RB

Hamlyn is an imprint of
Octopus Illustrated Publishing

ISBN 0 600 57241 2

Produced by Mandarin Offset
Printed and bound by Graficromo s.a., Cordoba, Spain

CONTENTS

AFRICA

NORTH AMERICA

South America

Antarctica

Australasia and the Pacific

EUROPE

ASIA

INTRODUCTION

The wonders of the natural world are so dazzling, so monumental, so arresting that they often seem to dwarf man's knowledge and achievements. Few of us can see America's Grand Canyon or the massive peak of Everest for the first time without finding ourselves lost in amazement and admiration.

From the earliest times man has dealt with his feelings of awe at the sight of nature's greatest works by crediting them with supernatural origins. Australian aborigines believe that Ayers Rock was given birth by Bulari, the earth mother, in the 'Dreamtime' before the earth came into being, while the Maoris of New Zealand believe that the geysers, hot springs and boiling lakes of the North Island mark the spots where fire emerged from the ground on its way to light a volcano to warm the legendary explorer Ngatoriorangi. Rivers, often the life-blood of the countries through which they flow, have been treated with reverence through the centuries. Hindus regard India's greatest river, the Ganges, as the goddess Ganga herself, her winding course symbolizing the twists and turns in the lives of men.

When European explorers first brought back news of the amazing sights they had seen, they had difficulty finding anyone who would believe them. Scientists scoffed at the idea that a snowcapped mountain like Kilimanjaro could exist near the Equator, and reports of the boiling fountains shooting from the ground in Yellowstone, USA, were greeted with ridicule. Now tourists by the thousand view the places once dismissed as travellers' tall tales, but nature has provided so many marvels that there always seems to be something new to be explored. After all, Angel Falls in Venezuela was discovered only in 1935, and the extraordinary Bungle Bungle range in Australia was almost unknown before 1982.

Modern geological studies have shown that many of nature's greatest spectacles are the result of the massive forces that shaped the earth many millions of years ago. Collisions of the plates that form the earth's crust have thrown up towering mountains; volcanic islands have grown from the lava vents in the ocean floor; glaciers have carved great valleys which were later flooded. However, more understanding of geological history does nothing to diminish the sense of wonder roused by the mountains of the Himalayas, the volcanoes of Hawaii or the fjords of Norway.

This book takes readers on an armchair meander through nature's marvels. Some have places in the record books: Hudson Bay, the largest bay in the world; Lake Titicaca in Peru, the highest navigable stretch of water; America's Rainbow Bridge, the largest recorded natural bridge. Some, like the limestone peaks of Guilin in China, or the perfect symmetry of Japan's Mount Fuji, have a beauty that has inspired poets and artists for centuries. Others, like Italy's Mount Vesuvius and Iceland's Vatnajökull, carry within them the power of destruction. Each has its own unique quality and ability to stir the senses, and many of them have been recognized as such an important part of nature's heritage that they are protected within national parks for the enjoyment of future generations.

Right: Mount Pumor, Nepal.

AFRICA

Amboseli Game Park, Kenya. Mount Kilimanjaro in the background

THE GREAT RIFT VALLEY

The Great Rift Valley is such a colossal fissure in the earth's crust that it is the only geological feature easily seen from the moon. It stretches 6,400 km (4,000 miles), beginning in the Lebanon in south-west Asia, running down the Jordan Valley, the Gulf of Aqaba and the Red Sea, then crossing Ethiopia, Kenya and Tanzania to Mozambique in south-east Africa. In all, it takes up nearly one-sixth of the earth's circumference.

The Rift was formed when subterranean forces split the land, separating the original supercontinent, known as Gondwanaland, into the present continents, which are now separated by oceans. Volcanic activity caused molten rock to pour from beneath East Africa, so that parts of its crust subsided. This weakeness developed into a series of earth movements in which the floor of the Rift Valley sank beneath parallel fault lines. Though the Rift probably began around 65 million years ago, the main phase of faulting dates back only 11 million years and more faulting has taken place since, forcing the shoulders of the valley upwards.

The complex forces that caused the giant tear have resulted in an enormous variety of terrain. The Rift contains around 30 active or semi-active volcanoes. Mount Lengai, standing at 2,740 m (8,990 ft) in northern Tanzania, has erupted 12 times since 1880. The last major explosion was in 1966, but since then the crater floor has been changing constantly, at one time containing a boiling lake, at another forming small new peaks. Nyamlagira, in eastern Zaire, sent down a stream of lava as recently as 1986

A chain of lakes runs through Kenya to north-east Tanzania, beginning with Lake Turkana, one of the most dramatic, 260 km (162 miles) long and nearly 30 km (19 miles) wide. Successive droughts have led to a lowering of the lake, which hundreds of years ago is supposed to have been connected with the Nile. Thousands of

crocodiles breed in its waters, feeding on an abundant supply of perch. Hippos bask in Lake Manyara in Tanzania, where the valley wall towers 300 m (984 ft) above the water and the rich bird life includes pelicans, storks, spoonbills, cormorants, fish eagles and Egyptian geese. Kenya's Lake Naivasha is also an important wildlife sanctuary with 350 different species of birds. Nearby is Hell's Gate Gorge, where a cross-section of the Rift Valley's wildlife can be seen: buffalo, antelope, zebra, hyenas and baboons. The lake waters are used to irrigate large plantations of carnations, exported at the rate of 200 million a year.

The Rift's savannah plains contain some of Africa's largest herds of big game. The extensive plains of the Serengeti National Park are formed from volcanic ash, which allows grass to flourish but does not provide a healthy base for trees. The game count is amazing: 1 million wildebeest, 1 million gazelle, 75,000 buffalo, 75,000 impala, 9,000 giraffes and 5,000 elephants. One of the world's great spectacles is the annual migration of the herds as they move in search of richer grasslands, in early summer and again in November. Wildebeest and zebra can be seen in columns several kilometres long, marching several abreast, stopping only to drink.

The width along the course of the Rift varies considerably. In Kenya (*see below*) the valley is only 40 km (25 miles) at its narrowest point, around the Kano plains, then it widens out to 320 km (199 miles), where the burning salt flats of the Danakil Desert in Ethiopia mark the northern end of the Rift before it enters the Dead Sea. The valley has provided many excellent finds for archaeologists. Its fossil remains go back thousands of years and at Olduvai Gorge near the Serengeti, the fossil beds are 40 km (25 miles) long and go down 100 m (328 ft). Anthropologists believe that the first human beings may have evolved in the region. Remains of the earliest known hominid have been found in Ethiopia's Afar depression and in Laetoli, Tanzania.

LAKE MAGADI

Lake Magadi is unique; its soda crust is so thick that, at the right time of year, there are places where a car can drive across it without sinking. Rainfall from the surrounding Rift Valley drains underground into Lake Magadi, 600 m (1,970 ft) above sea level in southern Kenya. On its way it is heated geothermally, and the heat accelerates the rate at which water can dissolve the chemical compounds of soda contained in the underground rocks. When the water surfaces as hot springs on Magadi's shores it is trapped in a 26 km (16 mile) long lake with no outlet and it evaporates quickly in the heat, with a temperature as high as 40°C (104°F). The evaporation process leaves behind on the surface a deposit of trona crystals, a mixture of sodium sesquicarbonate, sodium chloride and other sodium salts, and clays, that can be up to 30 m (98 ft) thick. For most of the year the surface is solid and shining white, though it can also take on a blue or pink hue according to the season.

The first European visitors to the lake comprised a geographical expedition from Germany in 1883, the members of which passed by without investigating. It was not until 1902 that two mineral prospectors realized the potential of the lake. At the time, it was estimated that Magadi held something like 200 million tonnes of trona. When processed, trona can be turned into soda ash, a valuable raw material used in the production of glass, as well as in the paper, textile and detergent industries. To exploit this rich new source, the Magadi Soda Company was formed in 1911. At first the isolation of the area brought enormous difficulties; special pipelines had to be built to bring fresh water to the site and a new railway line was needed before the large quantities of soda could be exported. World War I interrupted all the new company's plans and it was not until the 1920s that lucrative exports could get underway. Now production of soda ash stands at 275,000 tonnes a year, most of it exported to over 20 countries in Africa, the Middle East and Far East. In addition, about 40,000 tonnes of salt are manufactured each year, most of it sold within Kenya.

The 'company town' that has grown up beside Lake Magadi has over 4,000 residents and maintains its own hospital, power station, schools and even a golf course, with levelled earth substituting for greens. Apart from company employees and their families, the chief inhabitants of the area are the Masai tribesmen whose ancestors have eked out a living in the arid countryside for centuries. Long before the advent of the Europeans, the Masai made use of the trona deposits, mixing small amounts with tobacco to make a strong form of snuff. The Masai have always been expert at maintaining their cattle on the most inhospitable lands; but as any single family may own several hundred animals, finding sufficient pasture has always been a problem. A large amount of water from the Magadi pipeline has been diverted for the use of the local tribesmen, who still follow their traditional lifestyle, building simple houses from woven branches, plastered with clay and thatched with grass. Each encampment is fenced with a high thorn barrier to protect both people and cattle from night intruders.

For most of the year, Magadi, with its fierce temperatures and thick crust, offers little to tempt wildlife. However, in the rainy season the lake sometimes floods, with water rising as high as 1 m (3 ft 3 in) above the trona. In 1962 when the nearby lakes, the favourite nesting grounds of the flamingoes, were flooded, so that the food supply was diminished, over 1 million pars of flamingoes nested at Lake Magadi. Before the chicks were old enough to fly, the water had evaporated and the thick soda deposits became caked around the legs of the young birds, solidifying so that they were unable to walk. A huge rescue operation was mounted to return most of them to safety.

Lake Magadi may once have been part of a larger lake system that included Lake Natron and Lake Manyara. The springs and pools around each of these lakes contain closely related species of fish, and fossils of fish commonly found in the less saline lakes have been found some 12 m (39 ft) above the present level of Magadi. A unique species of fish, the *Oreochromis alcalicus grahami*, was discovered in the warm springs bordering Lake Magadi, flourishing in temperatures which are high enough to kill off many species. The heat of the water means that they are safe from most predators and they multiply very fast indeed. They have since been introduced to Lake Nakuru, which is 15°C (59°F) cooler, where they have adapted well and doubled in size.

LAKE NATRON

The salty waters of Lake Natron, in northern Tanzania, are the chief breeding grounds for hundreds of thousands of flamingoes, so many that the colour of the water is often obscured by a complete blanket of pink. Both Greater and Lesser flamingoes make their home here. The species can be distinguished by the colour of their bills: pink with a black tip for the Greater and deep red for the Lesser. The Greater flamingoes are taller; the Lesser far more numerous.

The lake owes its warm, salty water to the volcanic nature of the area, and the abundance of algae and tiny invertebrates that flourish in these conditions provides a rich supply of food for the flamingoes. As the Lesser is mainly vegetarian and the Greater is chiefly carnivorous, they can exist happily side by side. Both species feed with their heads inverted and the special structure of their bills enables them to filter the food from the water. The Lesser flamingo spends most of the day feeding as it moves across the lake, using its thick, fleshy tongue to pump the soupy water into and out of its mouth, while the hair-like structures on the upper and lower surfaces of the bill mesh together to exclude all but the tiniest organisms. The Greater flamingo tends to feed along the shoreline where it can stir up the mud and bring up the insect larvae, small molluscs and crustaceans that provide its staple diet. Its filter mechanism is much coarser than that of its smaller relative, allowing the algae to escape with the water. Both types of flamingo move their tongues and throats so vigorously that they can suck in and expel water three of four times every second. The salt water itself would be toxic for the birds, so they extract their food almost dry and drink at the fresh water streams on the edge of the lake.

The nesting site of the colonies of flamingoes was identified as Lake Natron only in the 1950s. They have never needed special regulations to protect them as they nest on mud flats out of sight of the shore and only the keenest ornithologist would risk burned and blistered skin by trying to reach them across water that sometimes reaches a temperature of 60°C (140°F). The flamingoes choose such isolated spots that local tribesmen still believe that the birds emerge fully grown from the waters of the lake.

The birds build a mound of mud as a nest, raising it up 36 cm (14 in) above the water and hollowing out the top. Both male and female sit on a single egg for as long as 24 hours at at time, folding their long legs over the nest. The eggs take 28 days to hatch and the chicks leave the nest after eight or nine days and band together in large groups, several thousand strong. Even so, the parents still manage to identify their own chick among the thousands and both continue to feed it by regurgitation for nine to ten weeks, by which time its special bill will have formed and it is able to fly. The conditions that keep the birds safe from man also discourage birds of prey, and flamingoes lose only a small number of their young.

Though Natron is their only regular East African breeding ground, the flamingoes move from lake to lake searching for food. When the waters of a lake rise considerably, it become too diluted to support the aquatic life necessary to meet the flamingoes' appetites and they will move on. However, there is often no apparent reason for one lake suddenly to be abandoned in favour of another. When they migrate they journey at night to avoid predators, flying with their necks stretched straight out and their legs extended behind them.

It is estimated that over half of the world's 6 million flamingoes live on the alkaline lakes in this part of Africa.

MOUNT KILIMANJARO

Johann Rebmann, a Swiss missionary travelling through what is now northern Tanzania in 1848, heard stories of a mountain crowned with something white, resembling silver but ruled by evil spirits, so that men who ventured on to its slopes found their limbs would stiffen and then they sickened and died. As he approached the mountain, Rebmann first thought its summit was enveloped in cloud. He then realized this was snow. However, his eye-witness account of the snow-capped Mount Kilimanjaro, standing only a few degrees south of the Equator, was greeted with disbelief in scientific circles. Its existence was confirmed only several years later, when other Europeans explored the region. A number of attempts were made to scale the mountain before a geologist, Dr Hans Meyer, reached the summit at 5,895 m (19,340 ft) in 1889.

The Kilimanjaro massif extends for 80 km (50 miles) and has three main volcanoes, all virtually extinct. The highest is Kobo which appears from a distance as a smooth dome but contains a crater (*see below*) almost 2 km (1¼ miles) across, outlined dramatically in the snow. The summit of all Africa, Uhuru Point, is on the crater rim and in the depression of the crater is a small ash cone which shows the residual volcanic activity. Outside the crater, glaciers descend to 4,260 m (13,976 ft) on the south-western slopes. Kobo is linked to Mawenzi, once the summit but now split and eroded, by the sloping 'saddle', a barren volcanic desert. Mawenzi seems to have been extinct by the time the first glaciation struck Kilimanjaro, but scientists have identified nine distinct lava flows from Kobo since Mawenzi died. A mild explosion, 200 years ago, left an elegantly symmetrical cone of ash around the crater and that was the last of its volcanic activity. The third volcano, Shira, the first to erupt but extinct for a quarter of a million years, is over 2.000 m (6,550 ft) below the summit. As many as 250 smaller cones

dot the slopes of the mountain, some filled with water, others choked with ash.

An ascent of Kilimanjaro is like experiencing a journey from the Equator to the Arctic, taking in desert, savannah, tropical rain forest and ice field. Above the 1,800 m (5,906 ft) contour line, all of the mountain is a nature reserve. The lower slopes are cultivated but above about 1,981 m (6,500 ft) is the forest zone, home of the colobus monkeys, with their luxuriant black and white coats and harsh cry. They make astonishing leaps from branch to branch in the trees, their long coats acting as gliding devices. The rarest of Kilimanjaro's creatures, the Abbot's duiker, is found here. Seldom seen because of its nocturnal habits, this small antelope is reddish brown in colour and about 75 cm (30 in) high at the shoulder.

The thick forest gives way to groves of heather trees, and dense tussocks of grass, with vegetation becoming more sparse as it reaches the moorland zone. Above 4,500 m (14,750 ft) the sweep of moorland gives way to the alpine zone, where the ground tempera-ture can reach 40°C (104°F) in the middle of a sunny day and drop below freezing for most of the night. In spite of these fierce climatic changes, 55 species of flowers have been identified as existing at this height. In the summit zone, with sparse rainfall, there is little life.

The southern slopes of Kilimanjaro are the most fertile, receiving rain from the south-east trade winds, and are the home of the Wachagga tribe, who grow bananas and coffee. As the rainfall is unevenly distributed throughout the year, they have developed a complex system of irrigation channels, with furrows extending for 16 km (10 miles) or more to bring water from the melting snows above. The volcanic soil of Kilimanjaro, light and moisture-holding, is well suited to growing high quality coffee and the irrigation methods have helped the Wachagga to become East Africa's most efficient producers of this commodity.

VICTORIA FALLS

As the Zambezi flows southwards through the undulating savannah of Zambia, its leisurely pace provides no clue to Africa's most spectacular waterfall lying ahead. For about 200 km (124 miles) above the falls, the Zambezi, at 3,500 km (2,175 miles) Africa's fourth longest river, flows though a wide, shallow valley and as its expanse widens, it is dotted with islands. The first intimation of the splendid sight to come is the cloud of spray, which can sometimes be seen from 60 km (37 miles) away, and when the falls are in full spate, the noise swells to a thunderous roar.

The earliest name of the falls was *Shengwe* (cauldron) but local African tribes, the Kalolo-Lozi, called them *Mosi-oa-tunya*, the 'smoke that thunders'. At one of the river's widest points, the water plunges into a deep rift in the basalt rock, lying directly across its course. The rift came into being some 150 million years ago and was eroded by water into its present shape. The water seems to explode at the bottom of the chasm and strong air currents catch the spray and send it soaring upwards in columns of mist, reaching as high as 300 m (985 ft). The mist catches the light, forming a series of colourful rainbows, and paler lunar bows form at the time of the new moon.

At is widest, the chasm extends over 1,700 m (5,577 ft) and at its deepest point it is 108 m (354 ft). During the flood season from March to May, the volume of water cascading down the rift is as much as 636 million litres (140 million gallons) a minute and its force is awesome. Its energy has been harnessed to provide power for the region by a 2,000 kilowatt hydroelectric plant, completed in 1938.

The crest of the falls divides itself into several small sections with little islands and rocky outcrops, and the dramatic torrent rages over the narrow precipice of the Devil's Cataract. The Cataract Island separates the Devil's Cataract from the 731 m (2,398 ft) wide Main Falls, which are split by a fissure. Then there is Namkabwa Island, still often called Livingstone Island, and the crescent-shaped Horseshoe Falls. Another promontory forms the Rainbow Falls, where the chasm is at its deepest. From the eastern shore extends the 101 m (331 ft) Eastern Cataract, often dry in the low-water season, and below is a hollow in the cliff known as the Armchair Depression, with its deep pool.

The outlet of the falls is a narrow gorge, only 64 m (210 ft) wide and 118 m (387 ft) long, where the full might of the river is channelled into an immense whirlpool known as the Boiling Pot. After that the Zambezi snakes through 72 km (45 miles) of steep-sided zig-zagging gorges, forming the Grand Canyon of the Zambesi. There are some 20 rapids in the gorge and adventurous white-water rafters run all but the six most dangerous. Once past the canyon, the Zambesi enters its mid-course, forming the border between Zambia to the north and Zimbabwe to the south.

Several vantage points on the cliffs opposite the falls, on the far side of the geological fault, offer magnificent views. One steep path leads a third of the way down the cliffside at Devil's Cataract and another to Danger Point, at the very edge of the cliff above the Boiling Pot. Another fine view of the falls is offered from the road-rail cantilever bridge, completed in 1905, which runs near enough to the falls for the rail passengers to feel the spray through the windows. Many visitors who arrive in the flood season expecting to see the falls at their best are disappointed: the spray is so all-engulfing that it almost hides the falls themselves, parting only occasionally to give a fleeting glimpse.

The missionary and explorer David Livingstone was the first white man to reach the falls, as he descended the Zambesi on his expedition of 1855. He had heard of the 'smoke that thunders' from the local people and approached them by canoe, landing on an island at the brink of the chasm. The falls 'had never been seen before by European eyes, but scenes so lovely must have been gazed upon by angels in their flight' he wrote.

Livingstone planted seeds of apricots and peaches, cotton, onions and coffee on the island, hoping to create a garden in a spot where the spray would keep it watered, but a hippopotamus trampled it into the ground. He also attempted to measure the falls, lowering a weighted line with a white cloth tied on the end. Such was Livingstone's reputation among the Zambesi tribes that the story of how the explorer had grown white wings and flown down into the gorge lingered on for many years.

THE AMPHITHEATRE

The Royal Natal National Park comprises 8,000 ha (19,768 acres) of awesome mountain scenery, but its most exciting feature is the massive half-moon of the Amphitheatre, its 1,500 m (4,921 ft) high cliffs slashed by huge, narrow clefts and punctuated by huge buttresses. This stretches for 8 km (5 miles) between the Eastern Buttress, 3,047 m (9,997 ft), and the Sentinel, rising 3,165 m (10,384 ft) in the west. The lonely plateau on the top is known as Pofung, the 'place of the eland'. From the beacon on the summit of the western buttress there is a panoramic view across South Africa, taking in Natal, the Transvaal, the Orange Free State and Lesotho.

Above stands Mont-aux-Sources, named by two French missionaries, Daumas and Arbausset, who were the first to climb its 3,282 m (10,768 ft) peak in 1936 and who named it for the number of streams springing from its plateau. Among them is the Tugela river (the name means 'startling' in Zulu), which plunges 850 m (2,789 ft) over the precipice of the Amphitheatre in a series of five cascades. The Tugela once marked the boundary of Zululand and there is a breathtaking view over its gorge.

The park, which acquired its 'royal' title when King George VI and Queen Elizabeth stayed there in 1947, stands at the northern end of the Natal Drakensberg, a mountain range stretching 1,000 km (620 miles) from the Cape to the northern Transvaal. There are various stories to explain the name of 'Dragon Mountain'. The most romantic is that it dates back to primitive times, when it was supposed to be the home of fire-breathing monsters. The discovery of the fossil bones of dinosaurs and enormous three-toed footprints lend credence to the idea. However, the Zulus, who might have been expected to know such folklore, call the mountains *Khuahlamba*, the 'Barrier of Pointed Spears', when carries no hint of dragons. The more likely explanation is that when the first

Voortrekkers came across the mountains in 1837, carrying their ox wagons in sections and looking for land in which to settle, they thought the mountains looked like the spines of a dragon and named them accordingly.

In the stretch of the Drakensberg south of the park is Champagne Castle, 3,375 m (11,072 ft), named after two climbers, who carried with them a bottle of champagne to toast their success at the top, but slipped and smashed the bottle on the rocks. A spur of mountains branching eastwards off the main range includes the 3,004 m (9,856 ft) Cathedral Peak.

In a valley dominated by the towering escarpment, a 3,000 m (9,843 ft) wall of basalt, is one of South Africa's oldest game reserves, the Giant's Castle, extending over 34,600 ha (85,495 acres) of grassy plateau, woodland and forested ravines. The reserve is a bird-watchers delight, where eagles and the rare lammergeyers are seen circling overhead and 140 species are recorded. In addition, there are about 600 eland, 12 species of antelope, including grey rhebok, reedbuck, mountain reedbuck, blesbok, oribi, red hartebeest, duiker and also baboon.

The lower slopes of the Drakensberg are made up of cave sandstone, pockmarked with hundreds of caves rich in rock paintings. They have never been precisely dated but the paintings, made by the Bushmen, or San, who once roamed through the whole of southern Africa, denote the earliest recorded history of the area. As the white settlers advanced, more and more of the Bushmen took refuge in the mountain caves and over 5,000 paintings have been found in the Giant's Castle Reserve, 500 of them in a single large cave. Many more have been found in the nearby Ndedma gorge and in the Sigubudu valley, near Mont-aux-Sources. The Bushmen were hunter-gatherers, using poisoned arrows and hunting their prey with great skill. Though their descendants still live in the Kalahari desert, their traditional way of life has all but disappeared.

THE NAMIB DESERT

The Namib is the oldest of all the deserts in the world, and also the most surprising. Its name comes from the Nama language, meaning 'a place where there is nothing'. Certainly there are few towns here and vast areas of the desert, with its mountainous, forbidding sand dunes, are completely uninhabited. Yet its situation and climate form a unique ecology and its flora and fauna have managed to adapt to the arid environment of the dunes.

The desert runs down the coastline of Namibia, in south-west Africa, its full length 1,600 km (994 miles) stretching from the border of Angola to the mouth of the Orange River, varying from 48 km (30 miles) at its narrowest point to nearly 150 km (93 miles) at its widest. The sand is yellow near the coast but glows red inland. The face of the dunes changes constantly at the whim of the wind: the Nama call the ever-sighing wind of the desert *Soo-oop-wa*. Lines of dunes, separated by troughs, run from north to south, diagonal to the prevailing south-westerly winds, reaching heights of 100–200 m (328–656 ft) and lengths of up to 50 km (31 miles). In the centre of the desert, near Sossusvlei, are the monster 'star' dunes, whipped high by multi-directional winds, and reaching up to 320 m (1,050 ft). Here and there, rivers of the past have carved ravines through the dunes, but the beds are normally dry; once in five years they may flow for a few days. Along the coast, the Namib may receive 1.3 cm (½ in) of rain a year in sudden, heavy storms, though there is often no rain at all. However, the cold Antarctic Benguela current in the Atlantic, which keeps rain from falling on the interior, also produces fog which can envelop the coast at night and penetrate as much as 50 km (31 miles) inland, creating a heavy dew. The plants and creatures of the Namib have developed ways of using the small amount of moisture to their best advantage.

Several species of tenebrionid beetles obtain all the water they need from the droplets of fog. One makes channels in the sand to catch extra moisture then makes its way back through the channel, absorbing water from the wet sand; another stands on a ridge of sand, its head lower than its back end, so that the drops of water run down a groove in its body to its mouth. The palmato gecko has webbed feet with which it can run across the sand and burrow into the dunes to keep cool, coming out at night to find food. The spider known as 'the dancing white lady', because of its elaborate display in the face of danger, builds tunnels in the sand, lining the walls wih webbing to prevent cave-ins. Other creatures that have adapted to the desert terrain are the *Aporosaura* lizard, which cools itself by lifting two legs and tail well above the hot sand, standing poised like a tiny ballet dancer, and the golden mole, a tiny, mysterious mammal identified in the area only in the 1960s, burrowing in the dunes and living on insect larvae and small reptiles.

The droplets of fog nourish grasses and succulents as well as the lichens – over 120 species, with more than 50 peculiar to the Namib. The most extraordinary of all desert plants is found not on the dunes but on the gravel plains of the north: the prehistoric *Welwitschia mirabilis*, some of them over 2,000 years old. Each plant stands about 1 m (3 ft) above the ground, its two leaves stretching out up to 3 m (9 ft) in an untidy, shredded tangle. They appear to absorb and store moisture from the fog but exactly how they do this is not known. When the naturalist Friedrich Welwitsch discovered them in 1859 he was convinced that these plants were 'the most beautiful and majestic that tropical southern Africa can offer'.

FISH CANYON

The mighty Fish Canyon slices through the arid land in the extreme south of Namibia, an unheralded and unexpected 85 km (53 miles).
long gash in the high barren plateau. The semi-desert countryside suddenly falls away into the 550 m (1,804 ft) deep canyon, its dimensions earning it a place second only to America's Grand Canyon in any list of the world's wonders.

The cliffs of the canyon provide clues to its origin. The lowest layer is ancient rock that was buried and metamorphozed through heat and pressure more than 1,000 million years ago. Dark sheets of solidified magma streak the lower rock face. Later, perhaps 700 million years ago, the rock came to the surface again and formed part of a seabed. The deposits from this time form a layer of sedimentary rock made up of water-worn pepples, cemented together by mineral action. The top layers of rock are made up of limestone, gritstone, and finally, sandstone. The beginnings of the 30 km (19 mile) wide canyon came with a volcanic rift in the surface of the earth and, with the coming of the Ice Age, glaciers prized the rocks further apart.

Though the Fish River has been involved in the process of cutting the canyon only for the last 50 million years, successive floodings, interspersed with droughts and strong winds, have scoured out the walls to their present width. In the dry season it is hard to believe that the river (see left) ever had the necessary power to do this. As it winds tightly on its 160 km (99 miles) course towards the Orange River in the south, its flow has been tapped by irrigation projects and for much of the year it completely disappears in the canyon, leaving only muddy water-holes behind. However, it can still turn angry and the little resort of Ai-Ais, at the southern end of the canyon, has been badly damaged by floods several times during the past 20 years.

Ai-ais means 'very hot' and the springs that bubble from the rock at 60°C (140°F) were discovered in 1850 by a shepherd boy searching for a wandering lamb. They are now used in medicinal baths and a swimming pool. There is a local story that two German soldiers escaped here during World War I and hid out for two months in the canyon; but as the same tale is told of other South African canyons, it may be apocryphal. From Ai-Ais, hikers can negotiate the canyon in four of five days, but parties are allowed in by permit only between May and August; the rest of the year intense heat and the possibility of flash floods make it too risky. The main viewpoint, at the northern end, is at a U-bend of the river, giving a magnificent view of the serpentine ravine.

Much of the land surrounding the canyon is a conservation area. Vegetation is limited to various types of thorn trees, wild tamarisk, rough grass tufts and succulents, with reeds and rushes around the water-holes. There is, however, sufficient food for a number of hardy animals, including antelopes, mountain zebra, and the wily, solemn faced baboons which can reach more than 40 years old. Baboons are the favourite prey of leopards and the traces of an occasional big cat are found here, but they hunt by night so that they are seldom seen. Ostrichs, which feed on seeds, insects and small vertebrates, exist in these semi-desert conditions. These large birds are the fastest creatures on two legs, capable of speeds of 50 to 70 km (31–43 miles) an hour, and the males can sometimes be aggressive. Klipspringers, taking their name from the Afrikaans words meaning 'rock' and 'jumper', can be seen leaping sure-footedly across the rocks. They walk on the tips of their hooves to give themselves a better grip and are found all through central and southern Africa, living at any height from sea level to 4,000 m (13,123 ft).

THE SAHARA DESERT

The Sahara is vast: its area of 8½ million sq km (3¼ million sq miles) makes it the largest desert in the world, and it is shared by ten countries. It is bordered by the Mediterranean Sea and the Atlas Mountains in the north, the Atlantic in the west, and the Red Sea to the east. In the south, the desert gradually merges into the savannah grassland of Africa's Sudan region, the Sahel.

The land of the Sahara lies lower than the rest of Africa, its seemingly endless, empty plains, ranging from 180 to 360 m (590 to 1,181 ft) above sea level. Though only one-fifth of the desert is sand, it is the sand dunes, stretching out over the horizon like a dry, rolling sea, that form the strongest image of the Sahara. The dunes change shape constantly; the top layers of sand are whipped into peaks and furrowed into troughs, alternately smoothed and ridged by hot, dry winds and baked by the sun. Pyramid-shaped dunes can reach a height of 230 m (755 ft).

Apart from the areas of continuous sand (*erg*), there are the more extensive plateaux where rocks have been eroded to leave a stony desert (*hammada*) and the plains of gravel (*reg*), like the harsh, boulder-strewn terrain of the Algerian Tassili plateau (*see below*). The Sahara takes its name from the plural of the Arabic word for desert and, within its boundaries, many regions have their own names: in the east the Tenere, or 'Land of Fear', and in south-west Algeria and north-west Mali the Tanezrouft, the 'Desert of Thirst', a featureless, waterless plain up to 1,450 km (901 miles) across – a place so lifeless that it was chosen as the first testing ground for France's atomic bomb. The highest parts of the Sahara are the Hoggar mountains in Algeria and the Tibesti mountains in Chad.

Daytime temperatures in the desert often reach more than 37°C

(99°F) and some of the highest temperatures ever recorded have been logged here. In the north, the hottest months are July and August, while the south sizzles in May and June. At night, temperatures drop dramatically. The wind blows day in, day out, bearing sand and dust along with it. In some areas, sandstorms rage for 70 days of the year. The winds can reach tremendous speeds along the plains and across the sand, where there is nothing to slow them down. Sandstorms, blinding and deafening, can whip up to 50 km (31 miles) an hour.

The driest parts of the Sahara have less than 2.5 cm (1 inch) of rain a year and sometimes go without any rainfall for several years at a stretch. The north has fairly regular winter rain and the south has some summer rain, but the rate of evaporation is so high that little water sinks into the ground.

The present dry climate dates only from around 3,000 BC, and there is evidence that in prehistoric times the fertile land supported buffalo, elephants and giraffes. Today's animals are more likely to be burrowing rodents, but gazelles inhabit the plains and wild sheep are found in the mountains. Though much of the desert is devoid of vegetation, in some areas grasses and members of the goosefoot and sunflower families manage to find a foothold. The most fertile spots are the oases fed by underground springs, as at Ouargla and Touggourt, with 2½ million palm trees between them. At El Goléa palms mingle with pines, tamarisks and eucalyptus. Tolga is one of several oases famous for its luscious dates. Over 70 kinds of date palms grow around the Sahara and their fruit has always been an important source of revenue. Some 100,000 tonnes of dates are harvested every autumn, about half of them the large, fat *deglet nour*, destined mainly for export.

The Sahara is gaining new importance as a source of oil and natural gas, and has rich reserves of minerals such as iron, copper zinc and lead.

THE HOGGAR MOUNTAINS

The bare hillsides of the Hoggar, or Ahaggar, mountains of the southern Sahara rise unexpectedly from the rocky plains, and grey-blue volcanic peaks jut out of the granite massif to form a dramatic outline. The remote, lonely landscape is unlike anything else on earth. These weird, other-worldly peaks are volcanic plugs, once formed in the exit pipes of volcanoes as magma forced its way through the rock and cooled. Over millions of years the outer layer has been stripped away, leaving the gaunt skeleton behind.

Among the highest of these mountains are Tahat 3,003 m (9,852 ft) and Assekrem 2,918 m (9,573 ft), and the surrounding plateau is littered with the lava and debris of ancient eruptions. The French writer Gautier described it as 'the desert of stones; of bare rocks or great plains of pebbles and gravel . . . stone swept and polished by the everlasting wind and veneered by the desert patina in all shades of dark red, brown or black'.

The Hoggar is a land hostile to man and its chief inhabitants have been the hardy Tuaregs, known as the masters of the desert. They live a mainly pastoral existence, herding sheep, goats and camels and they have always been known for their fierce independence and warlike disposition. At one time they dominated this region, controlling the routes between the oases strung across the Sahara. Few intruders penetrated the desert before the mid-19th century and little was known of the Sahara before Dr Heinrich Barth's five-year study expedition from 1850 to 1855. Towards the end of this century French interest in the region increased and the conquest of the Sahara began. First the Tidikelt Tuaregs were defeated, then the Kel Ahaggar Tuaregs capitulated in 1902. Once they were forced to accept French rule, the strong feudal Tuareg society to some extent

began to break down. However, the French administration boosted the power of the chief of the Kel Rela Tuaregs so that, through him, they were able to control a large area with only a small French presence.

The chief of the Kel Rela still has his seat at Tamanrasset, though his tented camp is further out is the desert, and still has widespread influence. Though the fierce drought of the 1970s forced many Tuaregs to leave the area for good, they can still be seen in the streets of Tamanrasset in their traditional blue robes (or the shiny, indigo robes worn for ceremonial occasions). No one knows the origin of the veils worn by the men, though they may have been simply a way of protecting themselves from blowing sand.

One of the first Frenchmen to arrive in the Hoggar after the conquest of the Sahara was Father Charles de Foucauld. A nobleman born in Strasbourg in 1858, he first came to North Africa as an army officer. However, his life changed completely when he be-

came a Trappist monk in 1890, and 11 years later he travelled to the Sahara as a missionary priest. First he lived in a tiny oasis on the edge of the sand dunes at Beni Abbes, where he became known for his selfless work. The French military governor of the Sahara persuaded him to move to the Hoggar and he built a small house in Tamanrasset, where his followers, the 'Little Sisters of Jesus', still work among the poor. He learned Tamalaq, the language of the Tuaregs, and even compiled a French–Tamalaq dictionary. The rest of his life was spent caring for the welfare of the local people. Ironically, though he earned the love and respect of many Tuaregs, he was shot by a Kel Ajjer Tuareg raiding party, during an uprising against France.

Foucauld set up a lonely hermitage high above on the Assekrem plateau. It is still maintained by two priests, the 'Little Brothers of Jesus', who spend their time in prayer and meditation. It is an ideal spot from which to watch the sunrise colouring the strange peaks.

THE NILE

'Egypt is the gift of the Nile' wrote the Roman historian Herodotus, and indeed the ancient Egyptians revered the river, knowing that they owed the prosperity of their great civilization to the fertility of the soil, enriched by the yearly flooding, which deposited rich red-grey silt throughout the Nile Delta. They believed that the floods were a gift from the ram-headed god Khnum, keeper of the Aswan Cataract, where they thought the river originated.

For centuries, the real source of the river remained a mystery and it took several 19th century expeditions to discover that two sources contribute to Egypt's greatest river. The White Nile has its beginnings in the Kagera River in Burundi, while the Blue Nile, which comes from high in the Ethiopian mountains, thunders over impressive falls (*see inset*) before the rivers unite at Khartoum. North of Khartoum an eastern tributary, the Atbara, joins the river and it is the Blue Nile and the Atbara which are mainly responsible for the annual flood. Monsoon rains and melting snow from the Ethiopian Highlands combine to swell both rivers from June to September and at this time of year the Blue Nile supplies around two thirds of the Nile's waters.

From Khartoum to Aswan the river flows along a narrow valley and through several cataracts, narrowing as it passes Elephantine Island (*see right*), with ruins dating back 4,000 years. Some of the cataracts were swallowed up when the Aswan High Dam was built in 1960, forming Lake Nasser, the world's largest man-made lake. The High Dam, 111 m (364 ft) high and over 3 km (2 miles) across, is the most ambitious of a series of dams which have meant that the Nile's flood-water can be retained for constant irrigation, thus making it possible for farmers to grow two or even three crops a year. The previous method of irrrigation, by which the flood-water was run into large basins divided by earth banks and allowed to drain away after a couple of months, leaving its silt behind, permitted only a single crop. As the dam was constructed and the waters of Lake Nasser rose, a number of archaeological sites were permanently flooded. The most important was the rock temples of Abu Simbel, one of the world's most remarkable ancient monuments, built in honour of Rameses II, during the 19th Dynasty. A tremendous rescue mission was mounted to move the temples, and they were sawn into manageable blocks of up to 20 tonnes and transported to a new site well out of the reach of the water, where they were re-assembled.

After Aswan, the river enters the main valley, lined with some of the most renowned sites of ancient Egypt, where holiday cruising has become big business. Among the main tourist destinations are Edfu, 2,000 years old and one of the country's best-preserved temples, the Temple of Hathor at Dendera, built in the 2nd century BC, and Luxor and Karnak, the site of ancient Thebes. Here the massive temple of Amun and the handsome sandstone Luxor temple stand on the east bank. On the west bank is the Valley of the Kings, the Theban necropolis, for kings of the 18th to 20th Dynasties, where 62 tombs have been excavated, including the fabled Tomb of Tutankhamun which was discovered with all its buried treasures.

North of Cairo the river fans out across the triangular lowland that forms the Nile Delta, extending around 160 km (99 miles) from south to north and with an area of 23,300 sq km (9,000 sq miles). Once the delta had seven branches but now there are only two main arms, the Rosetta in the west and the Damietta in the east. From its furthest source to its meeting with the Mediterranean, the Nile flows for 6,670 km (4,145 miles), making it the world' longest river. Its drainage basin is also the longest, draining about one tenth of Africa, though its area is less than those of the Amazon and Zaire basins.

THE RUWENZORI MOUNTAINS

The name Ruwenzori means 'rainmaker' and it is well-earned, for the range of mountains running for 100 km (62 miles) along the Zaire–Uganda border receives more than 228 cm (90 in) of rain every year. The peaks seldom emerge from thick, swirling mists (*see below*) and it is this, together with their strange animals and extraordinary plants, that have always given the Ruwenzori an eerie, romantic reputation. These were the fabulous 'Mountains of the Moon', mistakenly assumed until recent times to be the source of the Nile. They appeared on a map made by the Greek astronomer and geographer Ptolemy 1,900 years ago, who got the information from reports of travellers. Even earlier, it seems that Aristotle referred to them as the 'silver mountains'.

The snow-clad peaks stand less than 48 km (30 miles) from the Equator, the topmost being Margherita, at 5,109 m (16,762 ft) the third highest point in Africa. Unlike most African mountains, the Ruwenzori are not of volcanic origin but were formed from a plateau of ancient rock, isolated by major fault lines and pushed upwards – known geologically as a 'horst'. There are nearly 30 glaciers on the slopes and the permanent snowline begins at 4,510 m (14,797 ft) on the eastern side.

The lower slopes are covered with luxuriant tropical vegatation, thick with evergreens and tree ferns. At 2,400 m (7,874 ft) bamboo forest takes over, in its turn giving way to heathland at around 3,000 m (9,843 ft). On these higher slopes plants that would be unremarkable in gardens in many parts of the world grow to an amazing size. Giant lobelias (*see left*) grow to 6 m (20 ft) or more, likewise senecio, or groundsel, one of the world's most common plants. Heather trees, nourished by a soil rich in minerals and by plentiful rain, reach 12 m (40 ft), their branches draped in trailing moss. Elephant and buffalo are found in the grass and forest areas, while duikers (small antelopes) and leopard may be found almost up to the snowline. Among the strangest of the Ruwenzori creatures are the three-horned chameleon and the hyrax, looking a little like a rabbit but with hoofs in place of claws and a call that sounds like a shriek.

Cloud normally covers the mountains from about 2,743 m (9,000 ft) upwards, which may be the reason that they remained undiscovered until the late 19th century; expeditions passing within sight of the range may not have realized its height or seen its covering of snow. The explorer Henry Stanley saw them first in 1888 from the shores of Lake Albert, when a native boy in his party drew his attention to a mountain 'covered with salt'. At first he could hardly believe that what he was seeing was a real mountain; it looked more like a silver-coloured cloud. It was only when he looked below the silver to the blue-black base that he realized he was looking at a snowcapped mountain range. Stanley soon found that his glimpse had been lucky and that what he named the Ruwenzori were seldom so visible. When the clouds parted again, he described the sight: 'Peak after peak struggled from behind night-black clouds until at last the snowy range, immense and beautiful, . . . drew all eyes and riveted attention, while every face seemed awed'.

In 1906 the Duke of Abruzzi set out to map every mountain in the range. It was a carefully planned expedition which included four renowned alpine guides, several famous scientists and 150 porters. The duke and his party first climbed Mount Alexandra, at 5,105 m (16,750 ft), and then Mount Margherita; they form the twin summits of what then was called Mount Stanley and is now Mount Ngaliema. It was 26 years later that a Belgian expedition charted the glaciers and forests of the range. All the major peaks of the Ruwenzori have been climbed but there is much within the mountains that is secret and untouched; climbers and explorers still feel that they are journeying in an untravelled land.

NORTH AMERICA

Grand Canyon, USA

BRYCE CANYON

Over the centuries the Paiute Indians lived and hunted around Bryce Canyon, calling the area by a name that translates as 'red rocks standing like men in a bowl-shaped canyon'. The Indians revered all strange natural phenomena, and myths about the origins of the canyon became woven into their folklore. The brilliantly-coloured spires, pinnacles and domes of Bryce Canyon, the weird rock formations called 'hoodoos', are stained brilliant red and yellow by iron oxide, mauve and purple by manganese. They have been carved from the edge of a massive plateau by 60 million years of storms, melting snow and ice. Over that time, billions of tonnes of soft rock have been ground up and washed away in the Colorado River, and sculpted cathedrals, temples and fairy towers have been left behind. Many have fanciful names like Thor's Hammer, the Sinking Ship, the Alligator, the Chinese Wall and even Queen Victoria.

Byrce is not a genuine canyon but the ragged eastern edge of the Paunsaugunt Plateau (Paunsaugunt is the Paiute name meaning 'home of the beaver'). The Pink Cliffs of Byrce are the first level in the 'Grand Staircase' of southern Utah, standing at 2,800 m (9,186 ft) high. From here the land descends in a series of huge steps. Next come the Gray Cliffs, some 125 million years old, then the White Cliffs, some formations dating back as much as 165 million years. The Vermilion Cliffs and the Chocolate Cliffs, a reddish-brown colour, are even older. The foot of the Grand Staircase is the Kaibab Plateau on the north rim of Grand Canyon, its limestone more than 225 millions years old.

In the main Bryce Amphitheater, more than 32 km (20 miles) of trails wind down through the bizarre formations, wandering around the Queen's Garden and the Fairyland Loop, taking in the Hat Shop and the Silent City, snaking down the narrow passage through the cliffs of Wall Street and climbing a series of steep switchbacks along the Peekaboo Loop which, true to its name, provides unexpected new glimpses of this extraordinary landscape at every turn.

The range of elevation within Bryce means that the type of vegetation changes several times. The lower slopes support gambel oaks, piñon and juniper forests and the nuts and berries from these trees feed the mule deer, ground squirrels and chipmunks. The Paiute Indians used to use acorns to make meal and mashed up the seeds from the piñon pinecones to bake into cakes. The smaller mammals provide food for the coyote, foxes, bobcats and the occasional mountain lion, most of them spending the summer in the high country and moving to lower ground in winter. On the surface of the plateau grow the ponderosa pine forests, with cottonwoods and willow along the banks of the streams. Rainbow Point, at the southern end of the park, rises to 2,774 m (9,100 ft) and here ponderosa pine gives way to spruce, aspen, Douglas fir and white fir.

Among the most entertaining animals in the park are the prairie dogs. There are now several colonies in Bryce, but at one point these animals were in danger of being wiped out by farmers who considered them vermin. They are now, however, on the list of protected species. The small, grey rodents, members of the squirrel family, live in 'towns' that can cover several hectares (acres) digging tunnels up to 4 m (12 ft) deep. A mound of earth round the opening keeps out the rain. They can be seen standing on their hind legs on the edge of their burrows, 'barking' to warn the rest of the family of approaching danger.

Mormon pioneers looking for suitable homesteads in the mid-19th century must have seen the strange formations of Byrce but it was Major John Wesley Powell, who had already navigated the Colorado River through the Grand Canyon, who began a scientific investigation of the area in 1871. By then the Kanarra Cattle Company was grazing its animals on the plateau near the canyon. One of the earliest settlers was Ebenezer Bryce, originally a Scottish millwright, who arrived in 1875 and claimed grazing rights at the foot of the canyon. He summed it up as 'a hell of a place to lose a cow'. Bryce's simple log cabin still stands at the south end of the little town of Tropic, an early Mormon farming community.

The first tourist accommodation was provided in 1920 when Bryce's first postmaster began letting rooms in his home. In 1919, when the Utah legislature pressed for the area to be designated as a national monument, they planned to call it the 'Temple of the Gods'. By 1928 it was known as Utah National Park. Later, when the park was enlarged to over 14,165 ha (35,000 acres), it was decided to name it after its first known white settler.

THE GRAND CANYON

As Major John Wesley Powell began the hazardous first exploration of the Grand Canyon in Arizona in 1869, he wrote with some trepidation in his diary: 'We are now ready to start on our way down the Great Unknown. . . . We have an unknown distance yet to run, an unknown river to explore. What falls there are, we know not; what rocks beset the channel, we know not; what walls rise over the river, we know not'. Wesley's few small boats left Green River, Wyoming, in late May and emerged from the canyon's western end at Grand Wash Cliffs only on 30 August.

The canyon had been first seen by Europeans more than 300 years earlier, when it was sighted by a member of Coronado's expedition, searching for the Seven Golden Cities of Cibola. Of course more primitive peoples knew of the gorge 4,000 years ago: they left evidence of their sojourns in little split-twig figures, probably used in tribal ceremonies and preserved in the dry atmosphere of the cliffs. Then came the Anasazi, building dwellings in the canyon and cultivating lands on the rim until AD 1200, when they finally left, no one knows why. In more recent times, the nomadic Paiute Indians hunted here. They called the canyon 'mountain lying down' and had their own poetic names for the various plateaux of the rim: the 'little people', the 'place of pines' and the 'willow'. Though the Havasupai Indian Reservation lies within the canyon, the vast majority of human beings within this awesome gash across the landscape are tourists who come to gasp and marvel.

The Grand Canyon is 349 km (217 miles) long, 2,133 m (7,000 ft) deep at its lowest point and varies in width from 200 m to 29 km (656 ft to 18 miles). Its architect was the Colorado River, which

carved out the canyon as the Colorado Plateau was raised upwards. Before the Glen Canyon Dam was built in 1963, the river carried 500,000 tonnes of silt through the canyon every day; that has now been cut to a mere 80,000 tonnes.

In the rocks of the canyon, two billion years of history are laid bare so that geologists can read the story of the land in the layers of sandstone, limestone and shale. Each group of rock layers has its own subtle shade: grey, green, pink, then brown and mauve lower down. The youngest of the rock formations are 225 million years old. The canyon's sedimentary strata are rich in fossils, from primitive algae to trees, from sea-shells to the remains of dinosaurs.

The canyon's north rim, 2,500 m (8,202 ft) above sea level, is covered with spruce-fir forest while the south rim, 366 m (1,200 ft) lower, has pine and juniper. The contrast between the rim environment and that of the canyon floor is immense: down below is desert country, with summer temperatures as much as 6.6°C (20°F) higher

than those of the rim. The great range of vegetation supports an amazing range of mammals, including bobcat, mountain lion, porcupine, mule deer and coyote, with the desert floor providing a home for rattlesnake and chuckwalla. Around 200 species of birds have been recorded in the area.

Intrepid hikers and mule-back riders can experience the various climatic regions of the canyon in a single day. Mule trips are restricted to people weighing less than 90 kilos (14 stone) and riders need a good head for heights. Two trails lead down to the river from the south rim: Bright Angel Trail twists down 12.9 km (8 miles) from the Grand Canyon Village, and the steeper South Kaibab Trail descends 11.3 km (7 miles) from Yaki Point to a suspension bridge across the river. Only one trail, the North Kaibab, leads down from the north; 22 km (14 miles) long, it joins the South Kaibab trail at the river. A round trip from the rim of the canyon takes six to eight hours, even for the fittest walker.

The Painted Desert

The Painted Desert is a fantastic landscape of arid hillocks, stained with pastel hues and striped with bands of brilliant colour as though painted with an artist's giant brush. The shallow canyon of the desert sweeps across 240 km (150 miles) of north-eastern Utah. It is 16 to 24 km (10 to 15 miles) wide, bordered by the Little Colorado River in the west and Echo Cliffs in the east. In this low basin, over millions of years, successive floods have deposited layer upon layer of mud, gravel and volcanic ash, which have hardened as the water has withdrawn, to form sandstone and shale. This is known as the Chinle formation. Mineral compounds have soaked through the layers and have stained them with a rainbow of colours.

The whole area was eventually covered by an extensive inland sea and something like 1,000 m (3,280 ft) of rock was deposited on top of the Chinle formation. Then some 70 million years ago, an upheaval produced the Rocky Mountains and, at the same time, lifted the Chinle formation, with its overlying rock layer, well above sea level. Once the land emerged from the water, the sedimentary layers were exposed to the weather, to be baked hard in the sun and battered by storms and gradually wearing away to leave the eerie desert of coloured hummocks and low mesas. The process of erosion still goes on, gradually nibbling away at the soft rock so that, in time, the Painted Desert will disappear. In summer, the sun is so fierce that the ground becomes brittle and the crust cracks like miniature crazy paving. When the rain comes, with half the average annual 23 cm (9 in) falling as violent torrents, it washes away the top layer. The kaleidoscope of colour is at its most vivid after rain, but as much as 2.5 cm (1 in) of soil a year is lost in the floods, and the hillocks are constantly being diminished.

The area has yielded a rich harvest of fossils, from the stone trees of the Petrified Forest (*see overleaf*) to the remains of dinosaurs that roamed when the desert was still swampland. Bones, teeth and even fossilized faeces, found here in abundance, tell the story of the monsters of the past. The king of the mammoth reptiles must have been the Postosuchus, 5 m (16 ft) long with huge, serrated teeth and a bony crest running the full length of its body. The amphibious Metoposaurus was 3 m (10 ft) long, with a flattened head and long jaws, and probably preyed on the 6 m (20 ft) Phytosaurus, with its huge 1 m (3 ft) long snout. Two other reptiles found here were the 2 tonne Placerias, equipped with two sharp tusks, and the low-bodied Desmatosuchus, plated like an armadillo.

The first Europeans to see the Painted Desert were probably Spanish explorers of Coronado's expedition, which reached this area in 1539. But it is known that prehistoric Indians lived here from as early as AD 500. The Newspaper Rock, a huge sandstone block, is covered with their signs and symbols, impossible to interpret but probably used as a method of conveying messages. Nearby is the Puerco Indian Ruin, once a two-storey pueblo consisting of more than 100 rooms built around a central courtyard. Families supported themselves by farming, using springs that then ran from the surrounding mesas. When the springs dried up, they moved on, but archaeologists believe that the site was occupied for about 700 years until the 14th century.

The Hopi Indians have lived in the mesa-top villages overlooking the Painted Desert for nearly 1,000 years. Since they joined the Pueblo Revolt of 1680, when the Spanish were driven out of their territories, the Hopi community has remained closed and independent from outside cultures. Their simple homes are built in the adobe style and each village is run independently. Old Oraibi, probably inhabited since 1150, is the oldest continually occupied town in the USA.

THE PETRIFIED FOREST

A North American Indian legend tells of a goddess who collected logs to make a fire, hoping to cook a badly needed meal. To her dismay, the wood was damp and the logs refused to burn. She was so angry that she put a curse on them, turning them to solid stone so that they would never be able to burn – hence the existence of the Petrified Forest in north-east Arizona.

The first European reports came from military expeditions in the mid-19th century, when a Lieutenant A.W. Whipple described the place as 'where the trees have been converted into jasper'. It was a dull description for an area scattered with hundreds of fossilized logs, which shine and sparkle with semi-precious stones like a garden of gems. Once the railways penetrated northern Arizona word quickly spread and by the end of the century large quantities of the unique logs had been dynamited for gems or carted off by the truck-load to be crushed for commercial use. Protests by geologists led to the destruction being halted in 1906, when the area became protected by government degree. Now the removal of so much as a stone chip is strictly forbidden.

The Petrified Forest shares the Chinle formation history of the Painted Desert (*see. p. 42*). The trees found here are araucarias, closely resembling the native pines of today, and once they grew up to 60 m (200 ft) tall on hills as far as 150 km (93 miles) away. As they fell they were carried by flooding streams into the lowland basin where they now lie, to be buried so quickly and completely that they had no chance to decay. Though scientists admit that they do not fully understand the process of petrification, they believe that water rich in dissolved silica penetrated the tissue of the trees, forming deposits of quartz crystals, replacing the organic material but reproducing the details of the wood. Other minerals such as iron, carbon and manganese oxide added brilliant colours. In the bigger hollows of the trees the quartz crystals sometimes grew into large gemstones which were much sought after by 19th-century collectors.

Only some of the logs that collected here millions of years ago have been exposed; geologists calculate that many more are still buried down to a level of 90 m (300 ft). Most of those uncovered lie horizontally as they were carried along by streams, their branches and bark stripped off along the way. The few stumps are probably remnants of trees that grew along the banks of the streams.

The 37,835 ha (93,490 acres) of the Petrified Forest National Park actually take in several separate 'forests'. The Blue Mesa, named for the colour of the shale rather than of the trees, shows how erosion of the soft earth is still changing the position of the logs. Here, some remain perched on ridges like pedestals. As the ridge wears away they tumble further down the hills. The Agate Bridge is a single log, with over 30 m (100 ft) exposed, both ends still encased in sandstone. The ground beneath has been hollowed away so that it now spans a 12 m (40 ft) ravine. At the nearby Jasper Forest masses of log sections litter the valley floor. The breaks in the logs, which divide them into neat sections as though they had been chopped ready for the fire, probably began as cracks caused by minor earthquakes. These widened once the logs were exposed to the weather, and eventually separated into fairly regular chunks. The Crystal Forest once held large numbers of trees with clear and amethyst quartz crystals. These, however, suffered the attentions of 19th-century pilferers, so the most beautiful logs are lost for ever. The floor of the Rainbow Forest is strewn with chips of agate, onyx, jasper and cornelian, glinting in the sunlight like a jeweller's shop window. Here, too, are a collection of especially long logs, some as much as 50 m (160 ft) in length.

RAINBOW BRIDGE

President William Taft ensured the preservation of Rainbow Bridge by declaring it a national monument in May 1910. One of his successors, Franklin Roosevelt, hiked there and considered the arch, hidden away in a little-known corner of the Utah–Arizona border, the greatest wonder of the world. The largest known natural bridge on earth, it stands 88 m (290 ft) high and 84 m (275 ft) long. All official descriptions claim it is as long as a football pitch, tall enough for Washington's Capital building to sit comfortably beneath it and wide enough across the top – 10 m (33 ft) – for a two-lane road to run across it. Though the elegant line of the top of its arch may look fragile from below, it is 13 m (42 ft) deep. In Navajo legend, the pink sandstone arch is a rainbow turned to stone. For the Indians, rainbows form the guardians of the universe, so they considered it a sacred place, though for centuries they knew it simply as *Nonnezoshi*, the 'hole in the rock'.

In the first few years of the century, stories were passed around among the settlers and traders of Utah about a stupendous arch, situated in an isolated canyon. In 1909 a party consisting of W.B. Douglass, a government surveyor, Dr Byron Cummings of the University of Utah and John Wetherill, keeper of the nearby Oljeto Trading Post, set out to find the origin of the tales, guided by a Paiute Indian. After a journey of several days they finally reached their objective, and there are different stories about which was the first white man to see the bridge. One version insists that the honour fell to Douglass, another says that Wetherill agreed to stay behind so that Cummings could have the first view and that Cummings then halted to allow Wetherill to be the first to walk under it.

In spite of its speedy promotion to the status of national monument, few people braved the hazardous terrain to visit Rainbow Bridge over the next 50 years or so, and but for the advent of Glen Canyon Dam it would probably have remained one of the loneliest of natural wonders. The dam is part of the Colorado River storage project, a major source of hydroelectric power. When it was built in 1963 it created Lake Powell, 299 km (186 miles) long, the largest man-made reservoir in the world. The waters of the lake spread to fill the narrow Forbidden Canyon, along which hikers used to journey, so that it is now possible to reach the arch by regular boat excursion from marinas at Bullfrog, Hall's Crossing, Hite, San Juan and Wahweap, with only a short walk after landing. The adventurous can still approach by the hard way on a 22 km (14 mile) trail from the Navajo Mountain Trading Post, over slick-rock, across 1,829 m (6,000 ft) plateaux and through box canyons sizzling with heat.

Though natural stone bridges and arches may end up looking similar, only the bridges are formed by the erosion of water. Rainbow Bridge stands over Bridge Creek, a few kilometres above the meeting with the Colorado River. Here the stream followed a meandering course many millions of years ago and then, as the land gradually lifted, the water cut a deeper path through the sandstone. At a point where the stress almost circled back on itself it left only a very thin wall of rock. Periodic floods scoured away at both sides of the wall until eventually the water broke through. The stream then took the shorter course through the hole, which widened over the centuries to form a bridge.

The Natural Bridges National Monument, also in Utah, contains other outstanding examples of the same process of erosion, including the world's second largest natural bridge, Sipapu (the Hopi Indian word meaning 'place of emergence'), 67 m (220 ft) high and 82 m (268 ft) long.

METEOR CRATER

When a meteorite weighing thousands of tonnes struck the earth with the force of a multi-megaton hydrogen bomb in what is now Arizona, it left such a huge depression in the flat, featureless plain that the full extent of the impact can be appreciated only from the air. It measures 1,264 m (4,150 ft) across and is 174 m (570 ft) deep, its rim rising 40–49 m (130–160 ft) above the surrounding desert.

When Europeans discovered the crater in 1871, the favourite theory was that it was caused by volcanic activity. It was a Philadelphia mining engineer, Daniel Moreau Barringer, who first suspected that it was the result of meteor impact. He bought the land and began a series of scientific studies which showed that the crater walls were composed of sandstone and limestone, so that they were sedimentary, not volcanic. Barringer expected to discover a large section of the original meteorite. Thousands of pieces of meteoric iron were found in the vicinity, though few within the crater itself, and some weighed as much as 45 kg (100 lb), but no large body of metal was found. Barringer was forced to conclude that the meteor exploded on impact rather than burying itself. Drilling in the crater bed revealed crushed and fused sandstone down to a depth of 189 m (620 ft); beyond that the sandstone was undisturbed. Some of the shattered blocks of rock found for several kilometres (miles) around weighed as much as 4,000 tonnes. Scientists have concluded that the meteor was travelling at a speed of around 48,279 km/h (30,000 miles per hour) and that its impact would have destroyed all flora and fauna within a 160 km (100 mile) area. Estimates of the date of the impact vary from 20,000 to 50,000 years ago.

Meteorites, the 'rocks from the sky', are pieces of extraterrestial matter heated as they enter the earth's atmosphere from outer space. Several million tiny meteorites fall daily but are vaporized on the journey. The larger masses travel so fast that only the outer surface is vaporized, while the cooler core remains solid. If they are large enough, they may hit the ground and produce craters. Many meteorites contain radioactive elements, so that their age can be determined by radioactive means. The average age seems to be around 4,600 million years, the same age as the earth, suggesting

that they are part of the cosmic material from which the earth and the solar system were formed.

The earliest reports of stones falling from the sky are to be found inscribed on Egyptian papyrus from 2,000 BC. The temple of Diana at Ephesus contained a stone believed to have been thrown by the goddess, which was probably a meteorite. Another is the Sacred Stone of Mecca, revered by Islam. The oldest meteorite that has been positively dated is the Ensisheim meteorite in Switzerland, which came down in 1492. It was not until the late 18th century that scientists began to suggest that the falling stones might have a natural, rather than a supernatural, cause. In 1803, the first full-scale scientific investigation was made after a shower of several thousand meteorites fell at L'Aigle in France. Observers saw a flaming sphere in the sky, followed by an explosion like cannon-fire. A cloud hovered overhead and stones rained down as though shot from a catapult. The largest weighed 8.5 kg (18 lb 12 oz).

Since then, there have been some amazing falls. In Poland, in 1868, something like 100,000 small meteorites fell in the same shower. In 1908, the impact of a 40,000 tonne meteorite was heard 966 km (600 miles) away from the spot where if fell, in Siberia, causing hundreds of small craters and destroying 80 million trees. Meteorite blocks have been found all over the world: Mexico has three, weighing from 11 to 17 tonnes; a block of 60 tonnes was found in south-west Africa, and another weighing something like a million tonnes has been reported in Mauretania. More are being discovered all the time. In Antarctica, many emerge as glaciers shrink, and in an area of New Mexico where strong winds blow away the soil, 90 have come to light.

At least 80 large-impact craters have been identified, though some are badly eroded. The Arizona crater is the largest known impact crater, the second largest being at Wolf Creek in Australia, discovered in 1947 and measuring 850 m (2,789 ft). Many impact craters have been seen on the planets Mars and Mercury and on the moon. Meteor Crater has been important in scientific research because of its remarkable state of preservation. American astronauts have used it as a training site because its structure is similar to that of the moon craters. Here they have studied the geology of impact structures and crater mechanics and have rehearsed the techniques of collecting samples on simulated lunar walks.

THE ARCHES

The largest number of natural arches in the world to be found in any one place, at least 1,000, is in the Arches National Park in Utah. The most remarkable of these is the Landscape Arch, which holds the record as the longest arch in existence: a ribbon of rock stretching 89 m (291 ft) and standing 32 m (105 ft) high. The most photogenic is the Delicate Arch, 20 m (65 ft) high, perched precariously on the edge of a slick-rock bowl, its red rocky archway framing a view of the snow-tipped La Sal Mountains. The rest of the arches come in all shapes and sizes. Some, like the North and South Windows and the Double Arch, tower over the flat plain and are visible from long distances. Others, like the pretty little Sand Dune Arch, are hidden in secret side canyons.

The wonder of the arches began in the Pennsylvanian Age, 300 million years ago, when sea water rushed in to fill a basin caused by subsidence. Over many millions of years, countless floodings and evaporations deposited salt up to 2,450 m (8,000 ft) thick. About 150 million years ago, when the salt precipitation had more or less ceased, debris from mountain ranges collected on top of the salt, forming a rock layer up 1.6 km (1 mile) thick. Under this enormous weight the salt shifted, collapsing in places, bulging in others, and causing faults in the rock. Once water could penetrate deep inside, larger cracks opened up and the softer portions of sandstone were eaten away, so that narrow rock walls, or fins, were left behind. These fins are the raw material of arches. Water seeps into the cracks, freezes and melts again and rock begins to flake off. Flaking usually starts at the bottom and curves upwards, working through the fin until a chunk of rock tumbles out. The resulting hole eventually widens into an arch.

Geologists have tried to find a reason for the profusion of arches in this part of the country; they believe that this is the only area where the rock layer on top of the salt base is the pinkish-red Entrada sandstone, a brittle type of rock especially likely to fracture and flake in this way. Arches in all stages of development are found in the park. An arch is an arch only when it measures 1 m (3 ft) or

more; but there are plenty of holes, or 'windows', which will develop into arches over time. Then there are awesome expanses, with solid roofs of rock, and others, once standing proud, which have collapsed in a heap of rubble. The arches will not last for ever: Ribbon Arch is 15 m (50 ft) long, only 0.6 m (2 ft) across and a mere 0.3 m (1 ft) thick at its narrowest point, so its life expectancy is limited. Likewise, the Delicate Arch has an obvious weakness on one side and some day its fragile support will give way. Among other fascinating features of the park are the 'pothole arches', caused by water constantly dripping on the sandstone; Park Avenue, where a line of rocks have been sculpted into the likeness of a street of skyscrapers; and the Fiery Furnace, a labryrinth of sandstone fins which is unsafe to explore without the guidance of a ranger.

Much of the ground of the park is covered by cryptogamic soil, which looks like sugary brown sand. The word comes from the Greek meaning 'hidden marriage' and the soil is made up of mosses, lichens, fungi and above all, cyanobacteria, one of the earliest known life forms. Once the cyanobacteria become moist, they move through the soil, leaving behind a sticky trail that binds together grains of sand, soil and rock fragments to form a surface crust which performs several vital functions. It protects the ground from weather erosion; it provides nitrogen for plant growth; and it absorbs and stores water – particularly important in desert regions. Unfortunately the crust is highly vulnerable. The pressure of a foot can damage the soil, and it takes years to repair itself. The long depression left by a car tyre provides a channel which can be hollowed out by the wind and such areas may never recover.

Though various Indian tribes used this area as a hunting ground over the centuries, it was too barren to attract settlers, except for John Wesley Wolfe, a disabled Civil War veteran who built a ranch in 1888 and worked it with the help of his son. Against all the odds, they managed to run a modest cattle operation for 20 years. Their simple cabin, with its root cellar and corral, can still be seen.

The Arches became a national monument in 1929, during President Herbert Hoover's term of office, and was eventually designated a national park in 1971.

MONUMENT VALLEY

The Anasazi Indians, the 'Ancient Ones', lived among the massive sandstone monoliths of Monument Valley (*see right*) on the Utah–Arizona border, over 7,000 years ago, and remnants of their cliff dwellings, abandoned around AD 1250, can still be seen. They were superb artists, leaving evidence of their abilities in the abstract designs, animals and human figures carved into the red rock. Over 100 sites and ruins have been identified in this hot, barren setting, where survival must always have been a struggle.

Once the whole valley was covered by sandstone. This broke first into terraces which slowly split and wore into buttes and mesas, some towering as high as 300 m (1,000 ft). The surviving formations are capped by layers of triassic rock, more resistant to erosion than the surrounding sandstone, which was eventually flattened into the desert floor.

Many of the monuments have been given fanciful names, like the Three Sisters, Camel and Elephant Buttes and the Two Mittens, neighbouring buttes worn by chance into almost identical forms, like a giant child's mittens raised towards the sky. Merrick Butte and Mitchell Mesa were named for two miners who discovered silver deposits in the 1880s but were shot by Paiute Indians before they could enjoy their good fortune. As the sun moves round during the day, the formations change colour; sometimes gold or orange, at other times glowing red or dark brown. With the setting sun, the mammoth Totem Pole casts a shadow many miles long.

Monument Valley is part of the Navajo Indian reservation, though no one knows for certain when the Navajo first settled here. In 1863, following a long series of Indian raids on white settlers, Colonel Kit Carson was given the task of subduing the Navajo. He pursued a scorched earth policy, finally isolating them in their stronghold in the Canyon de Chelly and forcing their surrender. However, a small band under Chief Hoskinini was said to have escaped and found refuge among the monuments.

The less fortunate were rounded up and marched to Fort Sumner, New Mexico, where they were imprisoned for four years. The anger and bitterness of that time left long-term scars on the relationship between the Navajo and the US government. After 1868, the Navajos were returned to a reservation covering part of north-eastern Arizona and north-west New Mexico. Over half the land area of the reservation is arid desert like Monument Valley, so many Navajo have been forced to leave their families and work outside this area as migrant labour.

When film director John Ford found Monument Valley in the late 1930s and decided to use it as the location of his classic western *Stagecoach*, starring John Wayne, it was 322 km (200 miles) from paved highways and the nearest developed town. Ford visited the area after hearing stories from the silent film actor Harry Carey, who happened to find it when exploring Navajo country in the 1920s. Its wild grandeur fascinated him, though filming conditions could hardly have been more difficult, with the summers' searing heat, the winters' freezing cold, high winds and desert storms wreaking havoc with schedules, and most of the company having to camp out in tents. Ford negotiated terms with the tribal council and hired hundreds of Navajo as extras. The work was badly needed; at that time unemployment and alcoholism were rife on the reservation following a succession of hard winters. Following the success of *Stagecoach* (1939), Ford made several more films in Monument Valley and many directors have followed his lead. Motion pictures filmed here include *The Searchers* (1956), *How the West Was Won* (1962) and *The Legend of the Lone Ranger* (1980). The dining room at Gouldings Trading Post (first established in 1923) was specially built for the John Wayne film *She Wore a Yellow Ribbon*.

A Number of Navajo still live on the inhospitable lands of the valley. Their homes are the traditional little round *hogans* made of earth and logs, and some manage to eke out a living from herding livestock or growing crops in plots carefully sited and spaced to catch the run-off from the small amount of rainfall. Others serve the fast-growing tourist trade and work as silversmiths or weave the intricate blankets and rugs which are among the best-quality textiles produced by North American Indians.

The Navajo, who call themselves the *Dine* (the people), first arrived in the south-west around AD 1000 from Canada and Alaska. They speak a variation of the Athabascan tongue, a language so unlike any other that it was used as a code in World War II, a code no enemy could break. The Navajo nation is proud and progressive and is governed by a tribal council. Its self-governing structure includes courts and a system of tribal codified laws. Since 1934, the tribal council head-quarters have been at Window Rock, Arizona.

THE SEQUOIAS

The towering sequoias in the Sierra Nevada in California are the descendants of trees found on earth millions of years ago. They managed to survive in areas that escaped the last ice age and in modern times they are found only among the western slopes of the Sierra Nevada, where the conditions and climate have proved ideal for their growth. They are among the oldest known living organisms, dated by naturalists at well over 3,000 years old, which means that they took root when the Pharoahs ruled in Egypt and when the sarson stones were being dragged across Salisbury Plain to Stonehenge. They are true giants, their trunks averaging 8 m (25 ft) in diameter and many are over 9 m (30 ft). The king of the sequoias is the General Sherman, the largest of living things, with its branches bigger than most ordinary trees and its lowest limb 2 m (7 ft) thick. Its weight is said to be over 2,000 tonnes and it stands over 82 m (270 ft) high. The second largest is General Grant, standing 81.5 m (268 ft) high, with a maximum diameter of 12 m (40 ft).

The sequoias were named by Stephen Ladislaus Endlicher (1804–1849) after the Cherokee Indian who invented the first alphabet for his tribe's language. Sequoyah was so well respected that in 1828 he was elected to represent his people in Washington, DC.

The trees owe their remarkable age largely to their bark. Its high tannin content makes it extremely resistant to damage by insects and fungi, and gives it its distictive red colour. Its thickness, up to 0.6 m (2 ft), saves the trees from the attacks of animals and prevents disease from penetrating. When the Scottish naturalist John Muir visited the area in 1873 he wrote: 'Nothing hurts the Big Tree. Barring accidents, it seems to be immortal.' Storms tear off the branches and lightning strikes the topmost branches, but fortunately the effects are only temporary. After a forest fire, the trees simply turn black for a few seasons until they grow new layers of bark. One monster tree has a fire-hollowed hole the size of a room within its trunk, but it is still alive. Fires can even help in the growth of more trees, clearing space on the forest floor to allow fallen seeds to take root. When the big trees do topple and die, it is usually because the soil around their comparatively shallow root systems has eroded, cutting off the supply of nutrients and making them more vulnerable to storms.

It was miners, penetrating the Sierra Nevada in the California Gold Rush in 1848, who found and marvelled at the sequoias, passing on the word of their existence to the outside world. Unfortunately, the first reaction of those who saw the giants was to cut them down. Five men spent almost a fortnight felling one monster tree and stripping off the bark so that it could be reassembled and displayed at the Union Club on Broadway. The remnants of another ancient tree appeared at the Crystal Palace in London and was finally destroyed in the fire of 1866. The Centennial Exhibition in Philadelphia, brought about the death of another of the sequoias, leaving a stump large enough to be used as a dance-floor. The stump remains in Grant Grove, as a reminder of what might have happened to the whole forest without government protection. Loggers, too, found felling the sequoias a profitable business, though the timber trade was slowed down, mercifully, by the difficulty of felling the trees and cutting the timber into manageable sizes for transportation out of the mountains. John Muir, appalled by the destruction that was taking place, remarked bitterly: 'No doubt these trees would make good lumber after passing through a saw mill, just as George Washington after passing through the hands of a French Chef would have made good food.'

At last, in 1890, Sequoia National Park was established to ensure the safety of the trees and the nearby Kings Canyon, the steep-walled Kings River Valley, was added in 1940. The two parks are connected by the Generals Highway, which runs for 74 km (46 miles), passing Grant Grove, containing the General Grant and, as a sad contrast, the Big Stump Basin, where trees were felled by loggers. Also along the road are the Giant Forest, with the General Sherman tree and its imposing companions, the General Lee, McKinley, Washington, General Pershing and the Senate Group. The park roads and trails also give impressive panoramas of the Sierra Nevada mountains, formed by the tilting movements of a huge block of the earth's crust, where slow glaciers have gouged out 1.6 km (1 mile) deep canyons over the centuries.

YOSEMITE VALLEY

It has been called 'the incomparable valley', and the sheer walls, vast domes and streaming waterfalls of Yosemite Valley have fascinated visitors since its discovery in the mid-19th century. Even then it might have remained in obscurity, but for an Indian raid on a trading post in 1851. The raiders disappeared into the Sierra Nevada mountains and a battalion of soldiers under James Savage pursued them. One of the young soldiers, Lafayette Bunnell, was so enchanted by the beauties of Yosemite Valley that he risked capture to explore its beauties further.

Glaciers carved out the smooth U-shaped canyon of the Merced river, left intact granite crags like the slab-sided El Capitan (*see right, inset*) and the Half Dome (*see right*) rising above the valley floor 'like the walls of some celestial city', according to Scottish immigrant John Muir, who was to spend years campaigning for protection for Yosemite. Hanging valleys and natural waterspouts all round the valley create a spectacular natural display of cascades. They are at their best in May and June, as the snows melt; some diminish to a trickle in summer and others, like the Sentinel, Silver Strand and Ribbon Falls, disappear altogether. Yosemite Falls, where Yosemite Creek jets from its hanging valley, starts 739 m (2,425 ft) above the valley floor. The Upper Falls, 436 m (1,430 ft), and Lower Falls, 98 m (322 ft), combine to make a height ten times that of Niagara. Rainbows dance in the mists at the foot of the 97 m (318 ft) Vernal Falls.

The valley lies at the heart of the Yosemite National Park in eastern California, its altitude ranging from 600 m (2,000 ft) to more than 4,000 m (13,000 ft). Glacier Point gives the finest view of the park from a sheer cliff 990 m (3,250 ft) above the valley. In winter, when the road is closed, cross-country skiers make for the point to enjoy the sparkling winter panorama. Over 1,300 km (800 miles) of trails criss-cross the park, and there are many scenic areas. The rugged Tenaya Canyon was named for the powerful Indian chief pursued by Savage and his party. Tuolumne Meadows, the largest subalpine meadow in the Sierra, is carpeted by wild flowers in early summer. The Tioga Road, which crosses Tuolumne, had its beginnings as a mining track in the 1880s; it is California' highest road, rising to 3,031 m (9,945 ft) at Tioga Pass, and is accessible to cars only from mid-June to mid-October. Mirror Lake reflects jagged peaks in its clear, smooth surface. The lake is gradually silting up and, in a few years' time it will probably turn into a meadow. Once the Hetch Hetchy Valley was as grand as the Yosemite Valley, but with the building of a dam in 1915 it was flooded to a depth of 91 m (300 ft). The road to the reservoir runs through fine stands of white fir and sugar pine.

The Mariposa Grove, 56 km (35 miles) south of the Yosemite Valley, is the biggest of the park's groves of sequoia trees. The Grizzly Giant is 2,700 years old and deserves its name, with a height of 64 m (210 ft) and a base 10 m (33 ft) in diameter. The 71 m (232 ft) California Tree has a tunnel through the middle; evidence of the days when novelty was considered more important than conservation.

The Pioneer Yosemite History Center at Wawona, with its stagecoach, collection of historic buildings transported from various locations and dislays of pioneer crafts, gives first-hand experience of days gone by. Wawona ('big tree') has had accommodation for travellers since 1857, when Clark's Station was a simple coach stop. The rambling old Wawona Hotel, with its distinctive wooden verandah, was built in 1875 and is still functioning today.

The first recognition that Yosemite must be preserved for the nation came in 1860 when it became a state park 'for public use, resort and recreation for all time'. However, it was left to John Muir, who made his home in Yosemite, to launch a crusade for further protection from over-grazing by sheep and exploitation by timber merchants. Muir spoke and wrote with passionate eloquence, insisting that the mountains and lakes of the area were the earthly manifestations of God's splendour and had to be saved. God had protected the trees from all the ravages of nature for thousands of years, he said, but only the US government could protect them from the greedy. He foresaw that more and more people would need a retreat in the wilderness from the stresses of city life. 'Mountain Parks', he wrote, 'are useful not only as fountains of timber and irrigation rivers, but also as fountains of Life!' Muir finally won the day after conducting President Theodore Roosevelt on a camping trip through the valley, and the park was taken under national control in 1906.

SAN ANDREAS FAULT

The San Andreas Fault, together with its offshoots, is the most widely studied fault system in the world, a giant fracture between two of the major tectonic plates of the earth's crust. It is a 'living' fault, with movements still occurring along it periodically, and 20 million Americans live with the threat of earthquakes. The fracture runs for 1,125 km (700 miles) from Point Reyes, north of San Francisco, across the Golden Gate and through the centre of the peninsula on which the city stands, then south-eastwards to the hills behind Los Angeles and down to the Mexican border and the Gulf of California. Though much of the fault is hidden, in places it leaves a visible scar on the land.

Earthquakes happen because the Pacific Plate, on which San Francisco and Los Angeles stand, is grinding gradually northwards past the North American Plate. Scientists calculate that over the last 25 million years, this has resulted in a horizontal displacement of 282 km (175 miles). The current rate of movement is about 5 cm (2 in) a year and so long as the plates continue to slide past one another, all is well. However, in certain areas the plates tend to snag. Then stress builds up as they attempt to tear themselves free and eventually the slip results in a major shock.

At the time of the most famous earthquake in San Francisco in 1906, the movement was as much as 6.4 m (21 ft). The city's inhabitants had experienced quakes before, as recently as 1898 and 1900, but the low rumble heard in the early morning of 18 April 1906 heralded a colossal disaster. Three shocks were separated by a few seconds; the third was by far the greatest, its tremors being felt all the way from Oregon to Los Angeles, a distance of more than 1,000 km (620 miles). Buildings swayed and tipped, masonry showered into the streets, chimneys collapsed, church bells clanged wildly. Tramlines snapped and reared up from the road, short-circuiting in blinding sparks as overhead cables fell on them. All that remained of the newly built City Hall, supposed to be shock-proof, was the dome and the gaunt outline of the steel-framed tower.

Though the destruction was widespread, the initial loss of life was mercifully small. Then the fire began – small fires at first, but spreading to larger conflagrations as sparks ignited escaping gas. A

housewife cooking breakfast, not realizing that her chimney had been demolished, started the famous 'Ham and Eggs' fire that destroyed hundreds of buildings. Water mains were out of action, leaving the fire service helpless as strong winds fanned the flames, and for three days the fires raged out of control. Buildings were dynamited to stop the flames from spreading, but all too often they blew outwards instead of collapsing and the blazing debris started more fires. Many people were burned to death as they lay trapped in the rubble. The commander of federal troops drafted in to assist telegraphed Washington: 'San Francisco practically destroyed. You cannot send too many tents and rations. Two hundred thousand homeless.' By the time the fires had burned themeselves out on the fourth day, nearly 500 blocks of the city had been destroyed and the death toll had risen to 700.

In the southern half of California, the last major earthquake was in 1857, when the fault fractured for 349 km (217 miles) and in 1971 one of its minor offshoots ruptured; within ten seconds 1,000 buildings in the San Fernando Valley were destroyed.

The most recent reminder of the ever-present danger was the earthquake on 17 October 1989. Measuring 7.1 on the Richter scale, its epicentre was about 120 km (75 miles) south of the city, between Santa Cruz and San Jose. A 1.5 km (1 mile) stretch of the upper section of the Nimitz Freeway collapsed onto the lower level, crushing cars travelling along the highway in the evening rush hour and killing 63 people. The cities of San Jose, Santa Cruz and Los-Gatos were badly damaged, and in all more than 3,000 were injured. Buildings collapsed, water mains were severed, gas mains ruptured, causing a number of fires. Damage was estimated at $7 billion, making this the most expensive natural disaster in US history.

In spite of the long history of earthquake destruction, freeways, hospitals, university campuses and housing developments are built along the fault line. Though many of the specially designed buildings of San Francisco are expected to survive future quakes, high-rise blocks present a new danger, as sheets of glass are expected to fall from thousands of shattered windows and, as the 1989 experience showed, many of the city's elevated freeways will not withstand a severe tremor. Seismologists calculate that a quake on the scale of 1906 would result in 23,000 deaths.

THE PACIFIC COAST

The Pacific coastline of California and Oregon is one of North America's great scenic beauties. The angry waves of the storm season eat into the cliffs, carving them into sheer headlands and deep bays and leaving isolated rocks marooned in the surf. Winds blow sand-dunes inland and seabirds by the thousand wheel and shriek above cliffs where layers of marine fossils up to 40 million years old are exposed by the pounding of the waves on the rock face.

Along the Monterey peninsula in California, fierce winds have twisted cypresses into tortured shapes; one much photographed tree stands alone on a headland, bravely facing the ocean. The road from Big Sur to the peninsula is narrow and twisting, carved out high along the steep rock face. Point Lobos is at the top of a narrow strip of land jutting out into the ocean, and the California grey-whale, up to 15 m (50 ft) long and weighing up to 40 tonnes, is usually seen here in the winter months. Over 405 ha (1,000 acres) of land have been set aside here to protect the California sea otter and the endangered brown pelican. Robert Louis Stevenson lived for a time in Monterey in 1879, and Point Lobos is supposed to be the original of Spyglass Hill in his classic *Treasure Island.* He called the peninsula 'the finest meeting place of land and water in existence'. Above Monterey, the Spanish capital of old California, is Pacific Grove, where in winter millions of orange monarch butterflies cover the branches of the pine trees.

Beyond San Francisco, cypresses give way to Douglas firs. The granite peninsula of Point Reyes was created by the San Andreas Fault and the grassy dunes and wooded headlands are protected as a 29,948 ha (74,000 acre) national park, where over 70 species of mammals and 400 species of birds have been counted. Liquor smugglers from the Prohibition days used the hidden bays to land their cargo and the beaches have remained peaceful and secluded. Tidepools among the rocks teem with life; tiny fish dart backwards and forwards, crabs scurry across the rocks and seaweed sways with the current.

Further north, in Oregon, 36 state parks guard the seashore from development that might mar its wild grandeur. As the highway passes the state line, an even more rugged seascape unfolds. There

are few safe harbours and few beaches where it is safe enough to bathe. At Cape Sebastian cliffs drop 213 m (700 ft) sheer into the water. Nearby Gold Beach was named for the 19th-century finds at the mouth of the Rogue River and the surrounding countryside is dotted with old mine workings. South of Florence is an 80 km (50 mile) stretch of dunes, their golden sands constantly rolling inland, engulfing pine and spruce trees. Little gardens of grass and shrubs have been planted on the sand slopes in an effort to stabilize them. A herd of Stellar sea lions, named after the German scientist who identified them in 1741, arrive in September at their favourite spot, a set of caves a few kilometres north of Florence, wintering there and leaving for Alaska in May or June. They average 3.7 m (12 ft) in length and, when fully grown, are capable of attacking humans if they feel threatened.

At Agate Beach, near Newport, collectors can often find good gemstone specimens and the beaches between Tillamook and Coos are often dotted with moss and water agates, jasper and fossilized wood. The restless waves have created fine rock formations along the coast, including the huge monoliths called Three Arch Rocks, near Oceanside, and the Devil's Punchbowl, near Otter Rock, where waves boil angrily up in a rounded cauldron. From Otter Crest State Park, above the Punchbowl, there is a fine coastal panorama. The park was named for the sea otters, plentiful before the hunters killed them by the hundred for their fur.

The storms that assault the North American coast in winter give only a taste of the power of the Pacific Ocean. It was given its deceptive name by the 16th-century Portuguese navigator Ferdinand Magellan, in gratitude for a calm voyage from South America to the Philippines, when he enjoyed mild winds and watched the porpoises play. In a wild sea, winds can whip up savage waves over 30 m (98 ft) high. This is the world's largest and deepest ocean, covering an area of around 65 million sq km (25 million sq miles), larger than all the continents combined. Its average depth is 4,600 m (15,092 ft), though this is increased by various trenches. Most of these are between 6,000 and 9,000 m (20,000 and 30,000 ft), but the Tonga Trench reaches down to 10,882 m (35,702 ft) at its deepest point.

CRATER LAKE

The enormous cavity now filled by the blue, ice-cold Crater Lake came into being over 6,500 years ago, when a pocket of natural gas exploded beneath Mount Mazama, one of the great volcanic peaks of the Cascade Mountains in southern Oregon. The explosion was so powerful that it tore out the heart of the mountain, scattering pumice as far as 140 km (87 miles). Red-hot lava flowed for 50 km (31 miles), and as the rock drained from its core a yawning hole opened up beneath the volcano. Cracks in the side of the crater led to eventual collapse and the resulting caldera, or volcanic bowl, gradually filled with water to form the lake.

Local Indians have their own far more colourful version of Crater Lake's beginnings. Legend tells how the gods of the earth, determined to defeat Llao, the god of the underworld, once and for all, pursued him to his home on the 365 m (1,200 ft) Mount Mazama and fought a fierce battle, scattering flame across the mountains,

setting fire to the forests and raining molten rock on the surrounding countryside. When Llao finally disappeared down his secret passage into the mountain, the earth gods ripped up a mountain and hurled it after him. Its peak landed in the ground, blocking Llao's escape route for all eternity, its impact causing the crater that formed the lake. The Indians gave it a wide berth, believing that looking on the battleground of the gods was inviting bad luck, but today's tourists have no such inhibitions.

Crater Lake is about 9.5 km (6 miles) long and 8 km (5 miles) wide and its 589 m (1,932 ft) depth makes it the second deepest lake in the western hemisphere. The Great Slave Lake in Canada is deeper by only 24 m (80 ft) and there are only six deeper lakes world-wide. Multi-coloured lava walls up to 610 m (2,000 ft) high encircle the lake and a road runs around the rim, giving many excellent viewpoints. The smooth expanse of water is broken only by two small islands: on the western side is the cinder cone of Wizard Island, 232 m (760 ft) high, and there is the pile of lava debris known as Phantom Ship which seems to sail the lake like a ghost vessel. Like a number of other cones, hidden below the water

line, they are the result of volcanic activity since the initial explosion.

The lake was discovered in June 1853 by a young prospector John Wesley Hillman, whose party was searching for a lost goldmine. He called it Deep Blue Lake. It was 16 years later when the residents of Oregon gave the lake its present name. When an immigrant from Kansas, William G. Steel, first visited the lake in the 1880s he was so enraptured by its beauty that he devoted many years to preserving it from the depredations of settlers and prospectors. In May 1902, Crater Lake was established as Oregon's first national park.

Rainfall and evaporation are so well-balanced at the lake-site that the water level scarcely changes winter or summer. Though the lake water is very cold, never rising above 13°C (55°F), it has frozen over only once since records were kept. It is said to be 20 times purer than any tap water and its deep blue colour derives from its depth and clarity. This is because it absorbs all colours of the spectrum except blue and violet and these are reflected skyward. Little can live here and when it was first discovered, the lake contained no fish. Trout and Kokanee salmon, have been introduced, but scarcity of food means that they do not grow big enough to interest fishermen.

Forests surround the lake, with fine stands of ponderosa pine and Douglas fir, as well as lodgepole and whitebark pine, Shasta fir and mountain hemlock. Bears, bobcat, elk, coyotes, Cascade red fox and porcupine live within the park, and hawks and eagles circle overhead. Over 160 km (100 miles) of trails take visitors into the surrounding mountains. One of the most popular is Discovery Point Trail, leading to the spot where John Wesley Hillman stood for his first view of Crater Lake. There are spectacular views from the Watchman, 549 m (1,800 ft) above the water, Garfield Peak at 579 m (1,900 ft) and Mount Scott, the park's highest point at 2,721 m (8,926 ft). The rim is prone to avalanches and in only one place is it safe enough for a road to lead down to the water; the trail descends 213 m (700 ft) to Cleetwood Cove. A worthwhile side road leads to the dramatic Pinnacles, 61 m (200 ft) spires rising from the floor of Wheeler Creek canyon. To the north of the lake bleak pumice deserts give a stark reminder of the crater's dramatic beginnings.

YELLOWSTONE NATIONAL PARK

Three tribes of North American Indians, the Sioux, Shoshone and Algonquin, originated from the land bordering the Yellowstone River but, though they knew of the geysers and boiling mud holes of this part of Wyoming, they believed that they were the work of evil spirits and kept well away. When fur trapper John Colter, a member of the Lewis and Clark expedition of 1804–6, first explored the geyser basins his description of 'hidden fires, smoking pits, noxious streams' was laughed to scorn. However, local surveys mounted by the government after the Civil War authenticated his reports and the area was nicknamed 'Colter's Hell'.

Pressure grew for some method of setting aside this unique stretch of countryside for the enjoyment of future generations. There was fierce government debate, with a number of vested interests pressing for regular commercial development of the land, but the conservationists won the fight. The first national park was born when President Ulysses S. Grant signed the act that would preserve a tract of land in the north-west corner of Wyoming,

overlapping into Idaho and Montana. There were more battles to come: in the 1880s, for instance, the preservationists managed to defeat a powerful mining lobby demanding a railway line through Yellowstone.

At 8,992 sq km (3,472 sq miles) Yellowstone is still the largest of America's national parks and perhaps the most fascinating. A series of plateaux – Central, Pitchstone, Madison and Mirror – ranging from 2,132 m (6,995 ft) to 2,589 m (8,494 ft) above sea level, make up the park and these are in turn enclosed by rugged ridges and peaks rising to 3,655 m (11,991 ft). Within its boundaries, Yellowstone claims 10,000 hydrothermal wonders.

The most reliable of the many geysers is Old Faithful, which erupts on average every hour, pumping out a steaming tower of water more than 50 m (164 ft) high. Each of the park geysers has its own unique qualities. One erupts through a narrow cone like a nozzle; another bursts from the bank of the river; others send jets of water in several directions at once. Some display once or twice a day, others once a week; some last for minutes, others for 48 hours at a time; and activity varies over the years. The Norris Geyser Basin, named after Yellowstone's second superintendent, from 1877 to 1882, is one of the park's most active thermal areas and

visitors can explore the boiling pools, spurting geysers and hissing steam vents from the safety of boardwalks. The Artist's Paintpots are brightly coloured mud pools, the Mud Volcano spurts and splutters, petrified tree stumps stand where they died, their roots in acid water, and the banks of the Firehole River steam gently above the clear water.

North of the geyser area, the Yellowstone River has carved its own gold-hued Grand Canyon, 32 km (20 miles) long and 365 m (1,198 ft) deep. Powerful waterfalls thunder down its sheer cliffs: the Lower Fall at 94 m (308 ft) is nearly twice the height of Niagara Falls, while the Upper Fall is 33 m (108 ft) high. The river flows from south to north through cold, clear Yellowstone Lake, set at 2,357 m (7,733 ft), the largest US lake at such an altitude. At Mammoth Hot Springs, mineral-laden hot water, forcing its way up through the earth, has created tiers of limestone terraces, forming delicately coloured pools. As much as two tonnes of limestone is brought to the surface each day, so the terraces are growing and changing all the time.

The park's forests and meadows are dotted with elk and antelope; bison roam the eastern ranges; and the Hayden Valley and the Lewis River are favourite haunts of moose. In the north-east of the park the Lamar Valley is good game-spotting territory, frequented by coyotes, bighorn, pronghorn, elk and moose. The most dangerous of the park's animals is the grizzly bear. There was a time when bears were seen daily on the roads of the park, accepting tidbits from motorists and posing for photographs. Once they lost all fear of humans they became a danger and for some years now there has been a concerted effort to discourage them from frequenting the populated areas of the park. However, there are still accidents, even deaths, when unwary hikers or campers meet up with bears.

In the summer of 1988, disaster struck Yellowstone when heat and drought, coupled with high winds, set the scene for wide-ranging forest fires. There was no hope of controlling them and almost 405,000 ha (1 million acres) were damaged. Over 227,000 ha (560,000 acres) of the forests were blackened, but only about 300 big game animals died in the fires and the thermal attractions were undamaged. However, the land is resilient; experts reckon that, in its 10,000 year history, Yellowstone has survived at least 300 fires of similar range and intensity.

GLACIER NATIONAL PARK

In the heart of the Montana Rockies, on the northern borders of the USA, lies Glacier National Park, named for the massive ice sheets of ancient times that sculpted the peaks and valleys, then melted away some 10,000 years ago. Within its boundaries it contains 200 lakes, 30 peaks over 2,133 m (7,000 ft) and more than 50 glaciers, the largest of them Grinnell, covering 120 ha (300 acres), its ice 122 m (400 ft) thick in places.

A fine highway, romantically called 'Going-to-the-Sun', is 80 km (50 miles) long from east to west across the centre of the park, running through a dazzling vista of mountain, valley and forest scenery. The road skirts St Mary Lake and heads towards the peaks of the Lewis Range. The first turnout from the highway gives a view of the Triple Divide Peak, from where streams formed by melting snow and ice flow in three directions, reaching the Pacific, the Arctic and the Gulf of Mexico. Going-to-the-Sun crosses the Con-

tinental Divide at the 2,030 m (6,664 ft) Logan Pass and then winds north alongside the towering and magnificent Garden Wall and descends to Lake McDonald, the largest of the park's lakes.

Near St Mary Lake, the road crosses the Lewis overthrust, a huge fault caused when, some 65 million years ago, one vast mass of rock was pushed as much as 30 km (19 miles) to the northeast, so that the rocks above are hundreds of millions of years older than the rocks of the Great Plains beneath. Among the other notable geological features of the park are Clements Mountain, a typical glacial horn, its pyramid shape the work of at least three successive glaciers, and the steep-sided, semi-circular basins known as cirques (*see below*). The small cirque (or corrie) glaciers begin as snow patches, then as the ice thickens the force of gravity begins to move them slowly downhill. Year after year of freezing and thawing weakens the surrounding rock so that bits breaks off and become embedded in the glacier, which scours out the ground as it moves, leaving a hollow shape like an armchair.

Most of the park's beauties can only be experienced on foot, along some of the 1,127 km (700 miles) of trails. Hikers can wander

through alpine meadows carpeted with wildflowers in summer and along the bright yellow borders of glacier lilies that bloom along the melting snowline. Trails lead through valleys where every rock face streams with lacy waterfalls and along rock walls coloured green, yellow and red. A little way above Lake McDonald is a bed of fossil algae, a legacy from the time when the rocks were below the ocean. To the north, near the border where Glacier National Park adjoins Waterton Lakes National Park in Canada, are some of the highest peaks of the area, Kintla Peak at 3,078 m (10,100 ft) and Mount Cleveland, 3,190 m (10,466 ft).

The range of altitude within the park is such that a wide range of trees can exist comfortably; they include hemlock and spruce, subalpine and Douglas fir, red cedar, ponderosa and lodgepole pine. In autumn the changing colours of larch, cottonwood, aspen, birch and elder provide a photogenic display.

Over 100 species of birds have been identified, including the golden eagle, and around 60 species of mammals. Mule and white-tail deer, elk and moose and the smaller creatures like marmots, badger and coyote are commonly seen. Along the streams and on the borders of lakes live the otter, muskrat, beaver and mink. Mountain goats, actually a species of antelope, leap from rock to rock on the sheer hillsides. This is one of the only two remaining refuges for grizzly bears in the USA. Grizzlies, the world's largest carnivorous mammals, can weigh around 227 kg (500 lbs) and are wary of man.

The mountains were the hunting grounds for the Blackfoot Indians, as well as the scene of a number of battles with neighbouring tribes, long before the advent of the white man. Though some of the northern mountains were recorded on maps as early 1806, exploration began in earnest only in the 1880s, in search of a suitable railroad route across the Continental Divide. A route was built along the southern edge of the area in 1891 by the Great Northern Railway and it was the railway moguls, among others, who pressed for the creation of a national park, with an eye to the possibilities of increased passenger traffic. Glacier was declared a national park in 1910 and 22 years later it was joined with Waterton Lakes.

THE COLUMBIA ICEFIELD

The last remnant of the great ice sheet that once covered the whole of Canada is the Columbia Icefield, 390 sq km (150 sq miles) of ice and snow formed over thousands of years (*see below*), lying along the Continental Divide. Nine great glaciers originate here, their meltwaters forming rushing streams which eventually flow into three oceans, reaching the Pacific along the Columbia River, the Arctic along the Athabasca and the Atlantic by way of the North Saskatchewan, via Hudson Bay.

The early explorers and fur traders used a track through the mountains, which is now the Icefield Parkway, one of Canada's most scenic drives. The road was begun during the Depression years as a relief-work scheme, though the modern highway was completed only in the 1960s. The Parkway runs for 230 km (143 miles), crossing two 2,134 m (7,000 ft) passes, with fine mountain scenery all the way and more than 100 glaciers visible on the journey.

The road begins at Lake Louise, once called Emerald lake because of its vivid colour but later named in honour of one of Queen Victoria's daughters, wife of Canada's Governor-General. A little over 30 km (19 miles) to the north comes first of the Icefield glaciers, the Crowfoot, where three tongues of ice once reached down the mountain like a three-toed foot. In recent years one of the glaciers has receded so far that only two toes remain. Below the glacier lies Bow Lake, its still, cold waters reflecting snow-capped peaks.

At Bow Summit, its highest point, the highway crosses sub-alpine meadows and looks over Peyto Lake, fascinating because its colour changes with the seasons. In spring it is deep blue, but it changes to turquoise in summer as the meltwater from the glacier above carries silt into the waters. A few kilometres (miles) further north the Mistaya River has hollowed out a narrow canyon and gouged pot-holes in the smooth limestone walls. As the tall rock face of Mount Wilson looms ahead, the road drops down to the Saskatchewan River crossing, then climbs steeply again for a grand view over the Weeping Wall cliffs, where water from melting snow on Cirrus Mountain seeps through cracks in the surface and cascades down in a series of waterfalls.

At Sunwapta Pass the road enters Jasper National Park, established in 1907 and named after Jasper Hawes, a trapper who set up a supply post in the area in the early 1800s. Here two rivers flow in opposite directions, the Sunwapta flowing north and the North Saskatchewan flowing east.

The huge Athabasca glacier, 900 m (3,000 ft) thick in places, plunges down the valley alongside the road. Two hundred years ago the ice reached down to what is now the road but it has since receded and is still retreating by something like 10 m (33 ft) a year, leaving behind an expanse of rocky debris. In summer, snowmobiles take visitors out to the glacier, where they can walk on the ice and sample the pure water of the surface melt. Another tongue of the Columbia Icefield is the Stutfield Glacier, its two handsome ice falls hanging 900 m (3,000 ft) down the side of Stutfield Mountain.

Shortly before joining the Athabasca, the Sunwapta River (its name means 'turbulent river') bends sharply through a fault in the rock and plunges into a canyon. Even more impressive are the Athabasca Falls 23 km (14 miles) south of Jasper, where the full force of the powerful river is channelled through a narrow gorge.

A side road climbs towards Mount Edith Cavell. Originally called La Montagne de la Grande Traverse by 19th century traders, it was renamed after World War I, in honour of the British nurse shot by the Germans for helping Allied troops to escape from Belgium. A trail from the north wall leads to the foot of Angel Glacier, which takes its name from the outstretched 'wings' at the top, crossing the rubble caused by the grinding of rocks along the edge of the ice. Another trail leads past the glacier tongue to the pretty Cavell Meadows.

Locals like to call the mountain retreat of Jasper, a major tourist destination, the 'gem of the Canadian Rockies' and many beauty spots are easily accessible from the town. The Jasper Tramway runs 2,464 m (8,084 ft) up Whistler's Mountain, named for the whistling marmots living on its slopes, for a wide-ranging view of the Rockies. A hiking trail leads 185 m (600 ft) to the summit. To the east of the town lies Maligne Canyon, where sheer limestone walls plunge 50 m (165 ft), and Medicine Lake, where the water level varies widely from season to season. The variation is due to an underground drainage system but the early Indians believed it was the work of spirits and avoided the mysterious spot.

HUDSON BAY

The world's largest bay is named after the explorer Henry Hudson, who was cast adrift there in 1611 and never seen again. Hudson had long been seeking the Northwest Passage, a hoped-for short route from Europe to Asia, and in 1610 he sailed from London in the 55-tonne ship *Discovery* to follow up reports of a channel to the Pacific across North America. He spent so long sailing round the enormous bay looking for a non-existent outlet that he became ice-bound at the southern end and was forced to spend the winter there. Over the freezing months tensions mounted and Hudson quarrelled with some of his crew members. When the journey home was at last under way, they mutinied and Hudson, with his son and seven loyal sailors, was set adrift in an open boat.

The east coast of the Bay was explored two years later and the south coast was mapped in 1631, but the west side was fully charted only in the 19th century. The Bay is an inland sea 1,370 km (350 miles) long, including St James's Bay at the southern end, and 970 km (600 miles) wide. It extends deep into northern Canada and covers a larger area than the combined size of Italy and France. Several major rivers flow into the shallow Bay, which averages only 100 m (328 ft) deep, with a bed of sand, clay, gravel and mud. The climate here is severe, with midwinter temperatures averaging −29°C (−20°F), so that the Bay freezes over and the thaw only begins in late April. It is only free from frost for one fifth of the year.

During the 17th century, French interest in Canada grew because of the success of the fur trade. Two French traders, Radisson and Groseilliers, saw the possibilities of cutting costs by transporting furs to Europe via the Hudson Bay, rather than hauling them back through Quebec as decreed by the French colonial government. Their rich haul of furs convinced British businessmen that this could be a lucrative venture, and in 1670 Charles II granted a royal charter to the Hudson's Bay Company, which claimed exclusive trading rights over all territories draining into the Hudson Bay. The area became known as Rupert's Land, after a cousin of the English king. The company established a number of trading posts along the

shores of the Bay and for many years the fur trade prospered, though hostility between the English and French increased. Most of the trading posts were captured by French soldiers in the later part of the century but were returned to the Company by the Treaty of Utrecht in 1713. Later the North West Company was formed as a rival trading organization and bitter competition led to armed struggles before the British government merged the two companies in 1821.

One of the first ports established by the Hudson's Bay Company was Churchill, in northern Manitoba, taking its name from the governor of the company, John Churchill, later to become Duke of Marlborough. Today, Churchill is the Bay's only major port, though the winter freeze means that it can operate only between July and October. During the 20th century the fur trade has declined and wheat has gradually taken over as its most important export.

Above Churchill, along the western coast of the Bay, is the austere land of Keewatin. The small communities here, like Arviat and Whale Cove, were originally Company trading posts but now they are Inuit villages, populated by the Arctic people who have traditionally lived by hunting, fishing and trapping. The largest and most recent of these communities, at Rankin Inlet – originally named for a British explorer who came here in the 1860s – is the only one established by industry, when the North Rankin Nickel Mines Ltd was founded in 1955.

A strange story lingers among the Inuit that their ancestors once found a boat full of dead white men, together with a live child. They were undecided whether this white creature was an animal or a god but they called him Kabloona, the 'one with bushy eyebrows'. As Henry Hudson's most noticeable feature was his thick, bushy eyebrows, the belief handed down was that this was Hudson's son.

The search for the Northwest Passage claimed other lives, besides those of Hudson and his companions. British explorer Sir John Franklin first attempted to find a route from Hudson Bay to the Arctic Ocean in 1819. His third voyage began in 1845 in two ships, neither of which ever returned, and it was only several years and many rescue missions later that the skeletons of Franklin and his crew were found. They had died of exposure.

AURORA BOREALIS

The glowing, colourful light displays seen in the night sky of the polar regions, like these phenomena photographed in Manitoba, are known as auroras. In the northern hemisphere they are the 'aurora borealis', the 'northern lights', while in the Antarctic regions they are the 'aurora australis', the 'southern lights'. Though modern scienfitic techniques such as satellite and rocket experiments have been used to investigate auroras, they are still not fully understood. The theory that auroras appear when electric particles sent out by certain regions of the sun are trapped in the earth's magnetic field was first advanced in 1881 and since then Norwegian scientists have taken the lead in the study, foremost among them Professor Carl Störmer of Oslo. The same shower of particles produces magnetic storms and the two phenomena frequently occur at around the same time.

As the particles enter the atmosphere they start to glow and appear as coloured lights, often red, yellow, green or silver. Sometimes the lights take the form of regular patterns, sometimes they change both shape and colour at great speed, forming arcs that send out streamers turning into a moving, twisting curtain of colour. The display, which can last for several hours, often ends with great waves of light rising from the horizon before finally dying away.

The colours of auroras are produced chiefly by molecules of oxygen and nitrogen in the upper atmosphere: the yellows and greens come from oxygen and the red and violet, seen often at the bottom of arcs and curtains, come from nitrogen. Most auroras occur at heights of 89 to 129 km (55 to 80 miles) above the earth, though they can be as high as 965 km (600 miles). They are most often seen during the maximum periods of the sun's 11-year cycle of activity. The lights of cities tend to obscure the display and tall buildings block the horizon, so country people are far more likely than city-dwellers to see auroras.

Reports on auroras go back for 2,000 years and descriptions indicate that the display has always taken much the same form. The philosopher Seneca (4 BC–AD 56), tutor to Nero, says that 'the fiery recess of the sky is like a cave dug out of space'. In early times, people sought supernatural explanations; they saw the coloured lights in the sky as fires of the gods, or warnings of disaster. Medieval Scandinavians believed that the auroras were Valkyrie horsemen galloping across the sky, while in the Arctic they were seen as lights held by spirits to light the way for the newly dead. In areas where fine auroral displays are unusual, they can cause widespread anxiety: in England in 1938 many drivers were convinced they were witnessing a second Great Fire of London and in Washington in 1941 it was thought to be the beginning of a German attack.

A classic description of an unusually fine aurora was given by Fridtjof Nansen in *Farthest North*, published in 1898: 'No words can depict the glory that met our eyes. The glowing fire-masses had divided into glistening, many-coloured bands, which were writhing and twisting across the sky both in the south and north. The rays sparkled with the purest, most crystalline rainbow colours, chiefly violet red or carmine and the clearest green. Most frequently the rays of the arch were red at the ends, and changed higher up into sparkling green, which quite at the top turned darker, and went over into blue or violet before disappearing in the blue of the sky; or the rays in one and the same arch might change from red to clear green, coming and going as if driven by a storm. It was an endless phantasmagoria of sparkling colour, surpassing anything that one can dream. Sometimes the spectacle reached such a climax that one's breath was taken away; one felt that now something extraordinary must happen – at the very least the sky must fall.'

NIAGARA FALLS

Other falls may be higher or wider than Niagara but for sheer magnificence the world-famous spectacle of the mighty falls, shared by Canada and the USA, never disappoints. Niagara Falls lie about half way along the Niagara river's course, between Lake Erie and Lake Ontario. There the 58 km (36 mile) long river plunges down a gorge, divided by the little Goat Island into the American falls, 328 m (1,060 ft) wide and 51 m (167 ft) high, which has only 6 per cent of the water, and the thunderous Horseshoe Falls (*see right*) on the Canadian side, sweeping round in an 675 m (2,215 ft) semicircle. At the foot of the American falls is the Cave of the Winds, caused by erosion. Below the falls, the water rages through a series of rapids, culminating in the Whirlpool, where the chasm is only 91 m (300 ft) wide.

Scientists calculate that the falls came into being more than 10,000 years ago, when retreating glaciers at the end of the last Ice Age allowed water from Lake Erie, at 174 m (572 ft) above sea level, to flow down to Lake Ontario, which is 100 m (328 ft) lower, forming a seaward outlet for the western Great Lakes, which constitute half the world's fresh water. In the last 1.6 km (1 mile) above the falls, Niagara descends 16 m (52 ft), flowing towards the precipice with turbulent force.

The first European to gaze on the falls was Father Louis Hennepin, a member of French explorer Robert La Salle's expedition in 1678. He had heard the thunder of the water from Lake Ontario 40 km (25 miles) away and went to investigate its source. In the 18th century, this was a region of trading posts and frontier forts, and during the war of 1812 several battles were fought near Niagara Falls. The first bridge was built in 1835 and since the late 19th century the falls have become one of the world's greatest hydroelectricity generating centres. When Father Hennepin heard the thunderous roar, the volume of water over the falls was probably twice that of today and they can no longer be heard from Lake Ontario.

In 1803 Jerome Bonaparte, brother of the great Napoleon, brought his new bride by stagecoach from New Orleans to view Niagara and started a fashion that turned the area into the 'honeymoon capital of the world'. However, its popularity brought problems, with the banks of the river being swamped by hawkers and catch-penny amusements, which turned the whole area into a tawdry fairground. Eventually the State of New York and the Province of Ontario bought up the land on both banks and forced the booming commercialism back into the towns. Though Oscar Wilde insisted on remaining unimpressed, remarking drily that 'the wedding trip brings two disappointments, the second being Niagara Falls', few of the honeymooners who still favour Niagara Falls as a destination would agree with him.

Queen Victoria Park, on the Canadian side, gives splendid views of the falls and from the American side they can be seen to advantage from Prospect Point on Goat Island. Some of the most exciting views are from above, in one of the specially constructed towers: New York State Observation Tower on one side and the Canadian Kodak, Minolta and Skylon on the other. At Table Rock, visitors can stand on the very edge of the horseshoe, then descend to tunnels that give a closeup of the great sheet of falling water. *The Maid of the Mists* boat ride goes right to the foot of the the the falls: a noisy, soaking and memorable trip. At night, searchlights illuminate the waters in a rainbow of colours.

In winter, when the volume of water drops because so much is diverted to provide electricity, Niagara Falls can partly freeze over and the sight of great columns of spray rising amid the icicles is dramatic. In the early part of the century, crossing the river below was a popular pastime, which ended tragically in 1912 when the ice blocks disintegrated and three people were drowned.

Many have been tempted to pit their strength against the mighty waters. As long ago as 1829, someone called Sam Patch swam across Niagara twice and there have been many stunts executed since then. Barrels and car tyres have been used to protect the daring stuntmen (and some women) defying death in the hair-raising descent. An exhibition, along the river off the Niagara Parkway, displays some of the home-made craft used and gives details of the attempts. A surprising number ended successfully, including one involuntary trip over the falls by a seven-year-old boy whose family boat overturned upstream. He survived without so much as a broken bone. No one, however, has managed to achieve the adulation gained by the famous Blondin, who was the first to walk a tightrope across the falls in 1859.

THE EVERGLADES

The Indians call the everglades *Pa-hay-okee*, meaning 'grassy water', for through the vast expanses of sawgrass and reeds creeps a freshwater river 15 cm (6 inches) deep and 80 km (50 miles) wide, moving almost imperceptibly towards Florida Bay at the southern end of the state. Sometimes the marsh gives way to open water, and sometimes small islands known as 'hammocks' rise just enough to play host to trees like gumbo-limbo, mahogany and palms, growing in jungle-like profusion. On the western edge of the Everglades and along the Florida Bay are the most extensive mangrove swamps in the world. Mangroves, nicknamed 'walking trees' because of their above-ground root system, flourish where the fresh water of the glades meets the salt water of the sea. Their roots reach down to the water like long fingers, helping to stabilize the coastline, so that it can withstand violent wind and rain in the hurricane season.

The 'river of grass' may look still and empty but in fact it teems with life. Over 300 species of birds make their home in the Everglades for at least part of the year. White egrets and tall blue herons stand poised in the shallows, scanning the water for fish, and anhingas drive expertly after their prey. Then they perch on a log and spread their wings wide to dry, standing motionless for so long that they look like statues. Far less common are the large pink roseate spoonbills and the endangered woodstorks. Large turtles can be seen making their ponderous way through the water and the shy manatee, too often killed or maimed by motor-boats in open water, finds a refuge here. The best known inhabitant of the Everglades is the alligator, once slaughtered by the hundred for its hide but now plentiful again as a result of protective measures. These powerful creatures, which average 2 to 3 m (6 to 10 ft) long, can be seen lying in the water, only the tops of their heads visible, or sunbathing on banks. Often they congregate under bridges hoping for food from visitors – though feeding them is strictly forbidden. The females build 2 m (6 ft) high nests of mud and grass, where their eggs hatch after nine weeks. The baby alligators are light enough to lie on beds of water-lettuce leaves (*see right*). Crocodiles, far more dangerous to humans than alligators, are seen only occasionally, usually in the Florida Bay area. They are normally longer than alligators, with narrower snouts, and greenish-grey in colour. Only a few hundred survive in Florida.

In 1947, 566,000 ha (1.4 million acres) of the Everglades was set aside as a national park and various trails give a close-up view of several different environments. The Anhinga trail runs through Taylor Slough, a freshwater river that always has reserves of water, so that birds and animals gather there during the dry seasons and there is usually a good complement of alligators. Nearby is the Gumbo-Limbo trail, through a thick, tropical hardwood hammock decorated with ferns and orchids. Multi-coloured tree snails dot the trunks of many of the trees. At the *Pa-hay-okee* Overlook, an observation tower looks out over the large expanse of sawgrass prairie. Canoe trails wind through mangrove forests – red, black, white and buttonwood mangroves grow here – the lakes and freshwater prairies.

In the Seminole Indian wars of the first half of the 19th century, the Indians took refuge from white soldiers in the glades, where they knew they would not be followed. For some time after the settlers had moved into southern Florida their main aim was to see the region thoroughly drained and turned into productive farmland. Even when all such ideas were abandoned and the importance of the delicate ecosystem of the Everglades was recognized, problems remained. As farmlands and the ever-growing population of the towns has put more and more demand on water supplies, the Everglades has lost out. The natural balance has gone and, in spite of all modern efforts to conserve the area, pessimists believe that the Everglades is doomed.

CARLSBAD CAVERNS

In the south-eastern corner of New Mexico, nestling in the foothills of the Guadalupe Mountains, is the Carlsbad Caverns National Park, which protects the world's largest and most extraordinary network of caves. Over 250 million years ago a vast inland sea covered the whole area, and at its edge formed a fossil barrier reef. As the sea dried up the reef became covered in layers of sediment. Then, when a geological fault split the reef, rocks were forced upwards to form the Guadalupe Mountains. Water containing carbon dioxide seeped down into the limestone, dissolving it to form hollows which gradually widened into underground chambers and galleries.

Drops of water, each carrying a tiny amount of limestone, kept seeping through into the caverns, gradually solidifying to form stalactites hanging from the ceilings and stalagmites rising from the floor. In some places, these joined to form enormous pillars. Many are tinted by iron and other minerals within the limestone.

A great natural arch 12 m (39 ft) high and 27 m (89 ft) wide forms the entrance to the caverns and from there a steep path corkscrews down 252 m (828 ft) to the Green Lake Room, which takes its name from a vividly coloured pool. The King's Palace is a circular cave with draperies of sparkling cave onyx, and a natural keyhole in the rock leads into the adjoining Queen's Chamber with its 'elephant ear' formations, so translucent that a light placed behind them makes them glow pink. In the Papoose Room, a profusion of delicate stalactites hangs from the low ceiling. The most impressive cave, the Big Room, is large enough to swallow up 14 football pitches. In the shape of a cross, it measures 550 m (1,800 ft) in one direction and 335 m (1,100 ft) in the other. The great, cathedral-like ceiling arches up to 78 m (256 ft). Among the decorations of the Big Room are pools with limestone 'lily-pads', formations resembling snow-laden forests, the colourful Temple of the Sun and the magnificent rock column called the Totem Pole, 11.5 m (38 ft) high. Other fantastic shapes in the caverns are known as the Baby Hippo, the Veiled Statue, the Bashful Elephant, the Frozen Waterfall and the Devil's Den.

One of the higher chambers of the caverns is the home of

hundreds of thousands of bats. Though there are more than a dozen species of bat in the park, most are Mexican Freetails, spending the summer at Carlsbad, between April and the first hard frosts around the beginning of November, before returning to their homeland for the warmer winter. They have a wingspan of 28 cm (11 inches) and spend their days packed tightly together hanging head downwards from the ceiling and walls, anywhere between 9 and 24 m (30 and 80 ft) from the floor. At dusk they leave in search of food, hunting for insects along the Pecos River and the Black River. The bats can 'see' perfectly in the dark because they emit pulses of electronic frequencies well beyond the range of human hearing which bounce off anything in their path, and this enables them to avoid colliding with obstacles and to locate the flying insects that form their diet. Each bat can consume half its own weight in insects during the night, so crops for many miles around benefit from the removal of unwanted pests.

The evening bat flight is an unforgettable sight, with as many as 5,000 bats a minute erupting from the cave, spiralling counter-clockwise into the sky and climbing steeply over the crest of the hill and into the far distance. No one knows what wakes the bats and signals the beginning of the flight; every evening an audience assembles in the specially built amphitheatre at a set time but the time of the flight itself can vary by up to an hour and a half. First comes a whisper of movement, then a fan-like whirring in the air, then the bats come thick and fast, their outlines blurred as the thin membranes of their wings beat furiously, their flight gathering speed up to 48 km (30 miles) an hour. At dawn they will return, folding their wings as they dive into the mouth of the cave.

It was the great spiral of bats, looking from a distance like smoke, that led to the discovery of the caves by settlers arriving in the region after the Civil War. Following the 'smoke' to its source, they found enormous deposits of guano, or bat droppings, that had accumulated over the centuries to a depth of several metres. Guano is rich in nitrogen, a natural fertilizer, so mining claims were speedily filed on the caves. It was a young miner, James Larkin, who first explored the Carlsbad Caverns thoroughly and it was largely due to his efforts that the caves became a protected monument.

BIG BEND NATIONAL PARK

Big Bend National Park is a rugged sweep of mountain and desert cradled in an enormous curve of the Rio Grande river where it forms the border between Texas and Mexico, a remote inaccessible corner, far away from any main roads. This was once the floor of a primeval sea, where sedimentary rock was deposited over millions of years, until in some places it was 300 m (1,000 ft) thick. Through the rock the river has carved its awesome canyons. The longest is Boquillas Canyon, cutting through the Sierra del Carmen for 40 km (25 miles). Near the mouth of the canyon, at the top of a sand slide, is a small cave hollowed out by the wind which gives a superb view of the deep ravine. The most exciting is the narrow Santa Elena Canyon, (*see left, inset*), its walls so steep that the sunlight never reaches the water. The most isolated is Mariscal Canyon where a long, hard hike to the rim ends in a wide view of the chasm plunging 460 m (1,500 ft) below.

The rugged Chisos Mountains (*see left*) have an austere beauty, especially at sunset when the rock face glows red, changing to purple. They dominate the three ranges of volcanic mountains within the park, rising to a height of 2388 m (7,835 ft). Lost Mine Ridge gives an overall view of the rocky wilderness and from the South Rim there is a panoramic view over a good deal of Texas, as well as the mountains of Mexico to the south. The climate is fierce, with summer temperatures reaching 38°C (100°F) on the desert floor, at a height of 549 m (1,800 ft), rising as much as 10°C (50°F) between sunrise and mid-afternoon. Above, in the Basin, at 1,646 m (5,400 ft), it can be 9°C (15°F) cooler. Snow falls only once or twice a year in the mountains but occasional summer thunderstorms cause flash floods and washouts and send the water surging through the canyons.

The wild life needs to be hardy in this untamed country. White-tailed and mule deer roam freely, peccaries, badgers, skunk and beaver are plentiful and coyotes howl in the desert twilight. More menacing inhabitants of the park are tarantulas, scorpions and the occasional cougar, the graceful secretive mountain lion which feeds mainly on the mule deer. Four species of rattlesnake and the poisonous copperhead snakes are all found in Big Bend, though they are seldom seen in daylight. Cold-blooded creatures like the ring-neck snake and the alligator lizard live in the shade of the rocks; others, like the western collared lizard which darkens the colour of its skin to absorb heat and lightens it to reflect heat, have their own ways of adapting to the climate. More than 400 species of bird are found within the park, including turkey vultures, ground doves, painted buntings, lucifer humming birds and even the colimar warbler.

Dinosaurs once tramped through Big Bend, foraging tonnes of plant food, leaving their story in fossil bones. Prehistoric man lived in caves in the mountains some 12,000 years ago and 4,000 years later nomadic Indians camped here. Around AD 1200, the pueblo Indians built their homes in Big Bend. The Chisos, or 'people of the forest', who gave their name to the mountains, hunted here in the 16th and 17th centuries but were later forced out by the Apache. When friction with the white settles was at its worst, the Apache used the mountains as a refuge. In the late 19th century a red ore whch could be turned into quicksilver (the Indians had used it for years for drawing rock pictures) was discovered and mining flourished for 40 years. Ghost towns like Terlingua, near the Santa Elena canyon, are the only reminders of the boom years. The area has changed hands several times, at one stage belonging to Spain, then Mexico, then to the state of Texas, which finally ceded it to the US government so that it could be turned into a national park in 1944.

The Rio Grande river, which borders the 2,865 sq km (1,106 sq mile) park, has its beginnings as a mountain stream in south-western Colorado and heads south-eastwards into New Mexico. It runs along the Texas boundary for 2,092 km (1,300 miles). Once it crosses the border into Mexico, it changes its name to the Rio Bravo del Norte. Finally it reaches the Gulf of Mexico near Matamoros. Along its course, irrigation channels and dams, constructed to provide water for wheat, fruit and cotton-growing districts, drain off so much of its water that by the time it reaches Big Bend, the river is slow-moving, shallow and meandering. However, the canyons of the park bear witness to its past force, a reminder of why it was previously called the 'Grande' river.

SAGUARO NATIONAL MONUMENT

The most astonishing plant of the hot and lonely Sonoran desert is the saguaro cactus which grow as plentifully as trees on a fertile hillside. The Spanish conquistadores crossed the desert, which spreads over south-east California, south-west Arizona and northern Mexico, in the mid-16th century, and seem to have been unimpressed with the vegetation, for the recorder of the expedition, Pedro de Castaneda, summed it up as 'spiky' without further amplification. Spiky the saguaro certainly are, standing proudly up to 15 m (50 ft) high, their branches lifted towards the sky, and the sight of thousands upon thousands of them, dotting the barren slopes as far as the eye can see, is unforgettable.

The saguaro is one of the stem succulents, which range in size from miniature button cacti to these enormous plants, weighing anything up to 10 tonnes. The saguaro grows slowly, and takes 75 years to reach 6 m (20 ft) and to develop its first arms; it can afford to take its time as it may live for as long as 200 years. The thick, waxy skin covers a mass of pulpy tissue and a tough, woody skeleton; the skin is deeply grooved and dotted with sharp spines. The roots fan out in all directions, their extent at least equalling the height of the cactus. They give the heavy plant a firm foothold and will collect all the moisture available after the spring and summer storms. The saguaro's growth period comes after the rain, when it has absorbed so much moisture that its grooves fill out and its surface is almost rounded. An adult plant can take in as much as a tonne of water. If it then has to face several dry seasons, it uses the stored moisture, its girth gradually shrinking. The sharp spines play a role in protecting the plant; in addition to preventing damage by animals like the bighorn sheep, they give some slight shade for the exposed sections of the skin and cut the power of the hot, drying winds. In May and June, large creamy-white flowers appear in clusters at the end of the branches. These flowers, adopted as the Arizona state symbol, usually open at night and last only a few hours.

Perhaps only one in 3 million seeds produced by the saguaro

when the fruit ripens in July will manage to germinate; it needs shade, which is in short supply, and its most likely fate is to provide a meal for the birds. Even the seeds that do manage to take root will mostly be eaten by desert creatures in the first few months. Those that survive will probably only reach 13 cm (5 inches) in the first eight years or so of their lives.

The birds are not alone in finding the cactus useful for food; the local Indians eat the fruit and ferment the juice to make a strong alcoholic drink. Animals that are able to survive in the harsh desert terrain, like coyotes, peccaries and the occasional mule deer, are wary of approaching the spines but eat the fallen fruits.

It is quite usual to see the heads of small birds emerging from holes in the cactus stem as the saguaro provides a comfortable home for, among others, the Gila woodpecker and the gilded flicker, which drill holes in the fleshy stem, preparing them up to a year in advance so that the sap has time to harden around the hole, as a protective shell. Once inside, the young birds are safe from predators. When the woodpeckers have finished with the holes, other birds move in, such as screech owls, the tiny elf owls, flycatchers,

sparrow hawks, and an occasional cactus wren. Another desert creature, the packrat, munches its way through the flesh of the saguaro making long tunnels through the trunk without causing the plants any serious harm.

The 198 sq km (123 sq mile) Saguaro National Monument in Arizona was set up in 1933 to protect the stately stands of cactus within its boundaries. The monument is in two sections; to the west of Tucson there are plenty of dense, vigorous stands of cactus, while the eastern section, below the Rincon Mountains, has many of the larger saguaro. In the desert scrub section of the monument, where the cactus grow, temperatures rise to 38°C (100°F) in summer and the annual rainfall is some 28 cm (11 inches). As the land rises towards the Rincon Mountains, temperatures fall and rainfall increases, so the vegetation changes, first to woods of oak trees, then to pine forests and finally, near the summit of Mica Mountain, to fir forests. The wide range of habitat means that there are nearly 50 species of reptiles within the monument (including the Gila monster, one of only two venomous types of lizard in the world) and 200 species of birds.

SOUTH AMERICA

The Andes

AMAZON RAIN FOREST

The vast Amazon rain forest stretches from Brazil's Atlantic coast to the lower slope of the Andes. It covers more ground than the whole of Europe, extending across 7 million sq km (2.7 million sq miles). Its dense canopy of trees, up to 61 m (200 ft) tall (*see below*), is essential to the health of the world's atmosphere, as up to a third of its oxygen is released by the trees during photosynthesis. At the same time, by absorbing carbon dioxide, the forests prevent a build-up of this harmful gas in the atmosphere that would otherwise have serious effects on the world's climate.

Botanists have recorded more than 16,000 species of plants in the Amazon basin. In only 2.5 sq km (just over 1 sq mile), over 60 species of trees have been counted. Each type of tree may support 400 insect species. Giants like silkcotton, para nut and sucupira trees form the forest ceiling and beneath grow shade-loving trees, often festooned with orchids, ferns, creepers and bromeliads.

Forest mammals include tapirs, giant anteaters, armadillos and many kinds of monkeys, hunted for food by the Indians. Also used for meat is the capybara, the largest living rodent. The 1,600 or so species of birds include brilliantly coloured parrots, toucans, hummingbirds, scarlet ibis and jabiru. Near river banks and on islets, wherever the sun can penetrate, brilliant butterflies gather on tropical blooms (*see below, inset*). One study of a 1 ha (2.5 acre) plot found 217 different types of butterfly.

The forest Indians have lived here for centuries, their houses made from poles and branches and thatched with leaves, their simple lifestyle, based on hunting and fishing, offering no threat to their finely balanced environment. Before the arrival of the Europeans, there were something like 7 million Amazon Indians, but over the centuries many were taken into slavery and many more were driven out. Outsiders carried with them diseases to which the Indian had no immunity. Today there are well under 1 million Indians left; in Amazonia some of the best-known are the Kayapo of central Brazil, with a reputation as fearless warriors, and the Yanomano in northern Brazil and southern Venezuela who retain their traditional way of life.

Modern attempts to exploit the resources of Amazonia have had

a disastrous effect. Almost half the world's remaining tropical rainforest is in the Amazon but it is disappearing at an alarming rate; conservationists calculate that unless stringent protection measures are taken, the rain forest will have been destroyed completely by the end of the first quarter of the 21st century. Slash and burn clearance for agriculture leads to the destruction of 8 million ha (19.7 million acres) of rain forest in Brazil alone every year. Third World governments often claim that full exploitation of natural resources is necessary to give their people a better standard of living. However, this deforestation is often counterproductive. The forest soil is poor, and once the protection of the overhead trees is removed and the cohesive action of the roots is lost the ground is at the mercy of fierce sun and torrential rain. The topsoil then washes away and the earth becomes barren, unable to support any form of agriculture. Scientists working in the Amazon demonstrated that annual rainfall of 216 cm (85 in) will wash away only half a tonne of soil from half a hectare (1 acre) of the forest floor, but that once the trees have been removed, 45 tonnes is lost in the same amount of space. Wherever the terrain slopes, rain that previously would have been held in the ground washes down into the rivers, swelling them so that low-lying land is inundated. The high levels of the Amazon river in 1988 resulted in widespread flooding. The other major threats to the existence of the forest are the clearing of land for cattle ranching, to supply the US meat market, and logging, to meet the demand for hardwoods from the industrialized countries.

Conservationists argue that the loss to the world at large from this devastation is enormous. For instance, the plants found in the rain forest have already been of inestimable benefit to mankind, as something like one quarter of all medicines in common use originally derive from them. Many more are still to be identified and put to use, either as cures for disease or as new sources of food, yet at the present rate of destruction, several thousand species could be lost each year.

Deforestation is also likely to contribute to the problems of the 'greenhouse effect', as burning rainforest is the cause of anything up to one third of the world's carbon dioxide pollution, and carbon dioxide is the biggest single cause of global warming, which could mean serious changes in weather patterns and catastrophic floods in the next century.

THE AMAZON RIVER

More than 1,000 tributaries add their water to the Amazon river, draining an immense area of South America's tropical forest and collecting about one fifth of all the water that runs off the earth's surface. Rising in the Peruvian Andes, less than 190 km (120 miles) from the Pacific Ocean, it flows 6,400 km (3,977 miles) through Ecuador, Colombia, Peru, Bolivia and Brazil to empty into the Atlantic Ocean. It is the world's second longest river – only the Nile is longer – but it is the greatest in volume. When the river reaches the sea it discharges 220 cu metres (58 billion gallons) of water every second and dilutes the salinity of the ocean for over 160 km (99 miles) out to sea. Seven of the Amazon's tributaries are more than 1,600 km (1,000 miles) long and the longest of all, the Rio Madeira, runs for more than 3,200 km (2,000 miles).

Along its course, the Amazon goes by many names. When it begins in the snowy Andean mountains, at 5,250 m (17,224 ft), it is the Apurimac. It takes a steep downward course as it flows northward, is later called the Tambo and then, after its junction with the Urubamba, the river becomes the Ucayali, flowing on across the Amazonian floodplain. When still some 4,000 km (2,486 miles) from the sea it joins with the Maranón, the second of the river's main headstreams. At the point where it enters Brazil, the river is called the Solimões and it becomes the Amazon proper only near its greatest port, Manaus, where the jungle is at its thickest. It is here that the strange spectacle of the 'wedding of the waters' takes place. The black waters of the Rio Negro, which rises in Colombia to form part of the boundary with Venezuela, take their colour from an acid produced by decaying vegetation in the swamps. When they join with the brown waters of the Amazon, both rivers are flowing so fast that it takes several kilometres for the waters to mingle completely. The barely explored Xingu is the last major tributary to join the main river and marks the beginning of the delta, which spreads out to cover 320 km (200 miles).

Along its course the Amazon varies in width from a sprawling river 14 km (9 miles) wide to a comparatively narrow 1.8 km (just

over 1 mile) in some places. Ocean-going liners can navigate the river for 6,300 km (3,900 miles) as far as Iquitos in Peru, once a booming rubber town and now the major tourist gateway to the Amazon jungle. From the time when it leaves the foothills of the Andes, the Amazon is flowing across land that is, at its highest, only 200 m (656 ft) above sea level. The climate is hot, with an average temperature of 30°C (85°F), and wet, with 216 cm (85 inches) of rain in the delta and 178·cm (70 inches) in the central section of the basin.

The Amazon and its tributaries are rich in fish, with something like 2,000 different species, among them the brightly coloured small fish like the neon tetra and discus, which find international markets in tropical fish stores. Some of the best-known larger species are the giant catfish, stingray, piracura and the dreaded electric eel, which can give off as much as 500 volts. The notorious Amazonian piranha does not fully deserve its fearsome reputation; it is more likely to finish off victims already wounded and weakened than to seek out healthy prey. In addition to the fish, there are turtles, caimans and anacondas (giant water snakes), also freshwater dolphins and the gentle manatees (sea-cows), the creatures generally supposed to have given rise to all the myths about mermaids.

The mouth of the Amazon was first discovered by Europeans in 1500, but the Spanish expedition led by Vicente Yáñez Pinzón ventured no further than this. It was left to Francisco de Orellana, also a Spaniard, to journey along the river from Quito in Ecuador to the Atlantic in 1542. He was so impressed by the size of the river that he called it the Rio Mar, the River Sea, but this name was soon lost. Orellana claimed that his party had been attacked by a savage tribe of warlike women warriors, recalling the Amazons of Greek mythology. At the time the river and the surrounding rain forest seemed such a fearsome place that the whole region became known as the Amazon. In 1641 a Spanish Jesuit, Cristóbal de Acuña, who published *A New Discovery of the Great River of the Amazons*, described the river as 'one vast paradise'. In 1848 the British naturalist Alfred Russell Wallace made an expedition down the Amazon collecting evidence to support the theory of evolution. In 1853 he published *A Narrative of Travels on the Amazon and Rio Negro*, which added considerably to the body of knowledge about the area.

IGUAÇU FALLS

The legends of the South American Indians tell how the roaring cataract of the Iguaçu Falls was created when Taroba, son of a tribal chief, stood on the river bank imploring the gods to let the blind princess he loved see again. Their answer came with the ripping of a gorge in the earth, so that the river plunged into it. Taroba was carried off in the powerful water but the sight of the princess was restored and she was the first human being to see the falls. Like so many natural wonders the falls were revered by primitive peoples as a demonstration of the power of the gods, and thousands of years ago this was used as a burial place by Indians of the Paraguas and Tupi-Guarañí tribes.

Iguaçu, the 'Big Water', is twice as wide as Niagara, a thunderous horseshoe of 275 falls on the border of Brazil and Argentina. From its source in the Brazilian mountains, the Iguaçu river flows across the country's central plateau to plunge down an 80 m (262 ft)

precipice at the lip of the plateau. Shortly before the big drop the river spreads widely, divided by rocky islets into scores of separate cascades, around a wide, semi-circular sweep. They reunite to thunder down into the chasm of Garganta del Diablo (the Devil's Throat'), then the river rushes on in deep, narrow, rapids to the junction with the third greatest river of South America, the Paraná, 19 km (12 miles) below.

The Iguaçu Falls provide a wealth of different spectacles. There are cascades that leap from the precipice in one smooth, streaming fall. Others smash onto a midway ledge in a cloud of foam; yet more jump from rock to rock, creating hundreds of tiny rainbows. The fierce spray created at the base of the falls rises 30 m (100 ft) in the air, filling the chasm. The lush setting of palms add ferns, bamboos and trees twined round with parasitic orchids, brilliant begonias and hanging green mosses add to the stunning sight. Swifts dart in and out of the falls, roosting in the rocks at night, and two dozen species of butterflies add splashes of colour.

To fully appreciate the falls, it is necessary to view them from both sides and there is a natural rivalry between Brazil and

Argentina. Argentina insists that it has the best of the falls while Brazil insists that it has the best panoramic views. The changing angle of the sun throughout the day means that the Brazilian side photographs best in the morning while the Argentinian side is best after midday. The Iguaçu national park is divided between the two countries. On the Argentine side, three trails provide close up views of the falls and the surrounding jungle. The Circuito Inferiore circles the bottom of several individual falls and the Circuito Superiore leads round catwalks on the upper rim. A third path, the climax of the trip, leads to the awesome and deafening Garganta de Diablo. On the Brazilian side, a trail leads down to a give a stunning view of the chasm and three tremendous cascades. Here it is possible to walk far enough into the falls to get very wet. A boat trip takes the stout-hearted to a small island at the edge of the Garganta del Diablo.

The volume of water varies from an average of about 1,755 cu metres (62,000 cu ft) a second to a maximum of 12,750 cu metres (450,000 cu ft) when the river is in flood. The rainy season runs from November to March, so that the best time to see the falls at peak volume is in January or February, though the temperature may be around 38°C (100°F). Between August and October the falls are less vigorous but temperatures are lower and the orchids are in full bloom.

The nearby town of Foz de Iguaçu has expanded rapidly since the completion of the Itaipú hydroelectric dam, the largest in the world. Since it was completed in 1990 it has become a tourist attraction in its own right.

The Spaniard, Alvar Núñez Cabeza de Vaca, was the first European explorer to find the falls. In 1541 he named them Salto de Santa Mariá, the 'Falls of St Mary', but the original name of 'Big Water' proved more enduring. Jesuits visited the falls and began to explore the Iguaçu River, but in 1767 they were expelled from the colonies as a body by Charles III of Spain, who believed that the Catholic order was becoming too powerful. The ruins of one of the missions, San Ignacio Mini, stands at the junction of the Paraná and Pirapo Rivers. Established in 1632, it was once a prosperous settlement where as many as 4,000 converts lived a communal life, sharing the fruits of their labours.

THE ATACAMÁ DESERT

The Atacamá is the driest place in the world; an arid ribbon of land running for 956 km (600 miles) from the borders of Peru, down through Chile as far as Copiapó. The 'wet' areas are lucky to receive 75 mm (3 in) of rain a year, other areas normally have no rain at all. Parts of the desert went without rainfall for 400 years from the later 16th century to the early 1970s. Near the coast, where a little moisture comes from sea mists, there is minimal vegetation but inland, where the skies are clear, nothing grows. Though a few streams do trickle down from the Andes, only one is strong enough to reach the sea. The coastal cities are dependent on water being pumped for hundreds of kilometres.

The exceptionally dry climate is due to a combination of factors. The Peruvian Current brings icy water from the Antarctic, which means that the air on the surface of the ocean is colder than the air above. This causes plenty of cloud and fog, but no rain. On the other side of the Atacamá, the Andes form an effective barrier, preventing moist air streams from spreading from the Amazon basin.

It never rains in Arica, at the northern end of the desert. The town nestles below the Morro headland, fringed by sand dunes, and the weather there makes it a popular sea bathing resort. Once it belonged to Peru but Chile acquired the port as part of the spoils in the 1883 treaty, ending the War of the Pacific. Peru and Bolivia had been allied against Chile in the war and the same treaty gave Chile the Bolivian province of Antofagasta. This meant that Bolivia lost her outlet to the sea and this has been a bone of contention between the two countries ever since.

The ports of Iquique, Tocopilla and Antofagasta have heavy rain on average 3 times in 100 years. To the north-east of Antofagasta is the oasis of Calama, 1,850 m (6,000 ft) above sea level, and one of the few places in the Atacamá to be self-sufficient in water. It also has the world's largest open pit copper mine, providing Chile with one quarter of its export income.

The early Indians who inhabited the Atacamá have left a legacy of geoglyphs, or earth pictures, that has puzzled 20th-century scholars. No one has managed to produce a definitive explanation for the many hundreds of pictures adorning the desert in the Azapa valley near Arica, covering a mountainside at Pintados near Iquique and in many other locations. There are representations of animals and people, geometric shapes and patterns. The largest of all is the 120 m (394 ft) Giant of the Atacamá, also near Iquique, stretching across the single hill rising out of a flat, empty landscape. How long they have been there or who made them, forming the shapes with dark-coloured stone set in the sand, is a mystery. In Peru, similar markings are believed to date from somewhere between 400 BC and AD 900. There, the famous Nazca Lines were made by removing a layer of dark stone to reveal the light-coloured soil underneath and they are on flat land, so that the form and extent of the pictures can be seen only from the air. In the Atacamá, the geoglyphs are set on slopes, so that most can be seen in their entirety from a sufficient distance, but the aerial view is still the best. There have been many theories about the meaning of such lines: some believe they have an astrological significance, others that they were drawn as messages for Inca traders, a sort of earth diary. The most simple explanation is that they were an outlet for creative artistry of an ancient race. The true reason why people who must have been scratching a bare living from the desert should spend many years laying out hundreds of mammoth pictures is likely to remain hidden for ever.

THE ANDES

The Andes mountains form the backbone of South America, running through part of Argentina, Chile, Bolivia, Peru, Ecuador, Colombia and Venezuela. It is the world's longest chain of continuously high mountains, running for over 6,437 km (4,000 miles). Ten of its mountains stand 6,700 m (21,982 ft) or more high, the highest being Aconcagua, 6,960 m (22,834 ft). There are more than a dozen others reaching more than 6,000 m (19,685 ft).

The beauty of the mountains masks a terrifying power; the Andes lie along the boundary between two major tectonic plates and earthquakes and volcanic eruptions have often caused widespread destruction. Among the most famous of the volcanoes are Sangay, Tungurahua and Cotopaxi in Ecuador. Small quakes are so frequent that the Andean people scarcely notice that their furniture is rattling, but a major quake can cause terrible snow, mud and rock slides. The most disastrous of recent quakes, in 1970, shook 965 km (600 miles) of the Peruvian coastline as well as a large hinterland, leaving 50,000 dead and 800,000 homeless. In the high mountains, the ice cap of Huascarán had collapsed, sending an avalanche of several thousand tonnes of rock pouring down the valley at 320 km (200 miles) an hour. The town of Yungay, a flourishing ski resort, disappeared completely below the rocks and a dozen more towns were reduced to rubble. The death toll quickly mounted as rescue attempts were seriously hampered by the difficulties of getting help to such a remote and inaccessible region of the Andes.

Travel and transportation have always been a major problem in the mountains, with natural barriers resulting in communities being isolated from each other as well as from the outside world. The passes are narrow, steep and winding. In some places they climb 3,000 to 4,600 m (10,000 to 15,100 ft) and are blocked by snow for several months of the year. The Central Railway, which climbs to over 4,815 m (15,797 ft) above sea level in Peru, negotiating over 120 tunnels and bridges, is the highest standard gauge railway in the world. Rail lines running from the Pacific coast to Quito in Ecuador and La Paz in Bolivia reach more than 3,350 m (10,990 ft).

The Andes contain a wealth of minerals; they were brought near the surface of the earth by the mountain-building process, then the movement of glaciers worked on the topmost layers so that digging out the minerals has always been possible. In the period of the Spanish conquest, the gold and silver from the central mountains of Peru and Bolivia were most in demand. However, since the 19th century, other minerals have become more important. It is estimated that Peru has sufficient reserves of copper, zinc and lead to supply the world for at least a century. The main mining centre is Cerro de Pasco, the terminus of the Central Railway. The name Andes probably comes from an Indian word for copper, and there are other important mining centres in northern Chile and Bolivia, an area which is also rich in tin, zinc, tungsten and lead.

Though minerals are the most important Andean exports, most people who live in and around the Andes exist at subsistence level on the land, raising potatoes, maize, barley and quinoa, a hardy native cereal. The Indians are skilled in making the best use of the mountain land, and potatoes are grown at up to 4,300 m (14,108 ft) and barley up to 4,200 m (13,780 ft). Above this shepherds graze flocks of sheep, llamas and alpacas. On the lower slopes of the northern Andes coffee is grown as a commercial crop.

In spite of the rigours of life at such high altitudes, the Andes nurtured one of the greatest of ancient civilizations, the Incas. At the time of the Spanish conquest in the 16th century, the Inca empire was at its zenith. After widespread military expansion in the mid-15th century, the empire extended 4,828 km (3,000 miles) across parts of Columbia, Chile, Peru, Ecuador, Bolivia and Argentina. The capital was at Cuzco, the city said by Inca legend to have been founded by the first of their race, Manco Kapac, child of the sun god. It was laid out in the 30 years following 1438 and modern buildings stand on foundations quarried by the Incas, with the original walls visible in many places. Near the town lie impressive ruins, including the fort of Sacsayhuaman, its huge, zigzag walls constructed from boulders weighing as much as 300 tonnes, and Ollantaytambo, its high terraces built on the steep hillside. The outstanding Inca site is the 'lost city' of Machu Picchu, set high in the mountains and never found by the Spanish invaders. It became known to the outside world only after American historian Hiram Bingham discovered the overgrown buildings in 1911.

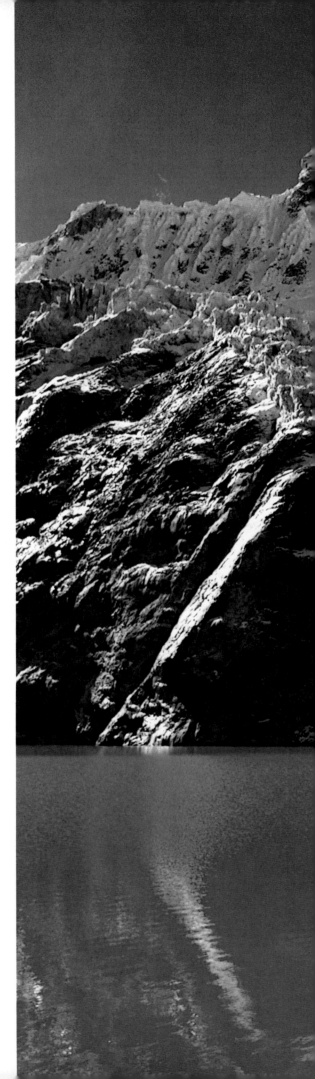

LAKE TITICACA

The dark blue waters of Lake Titicaca stretch along the borders of Peru and Bolivia like a huge inland sea, situated on the Andean Altiplano, a windswept plateau between ranges of mountains. On its north-east shore, snowy peaks rise to a height of 6,401 m (21,000 ft). The plateau is so high that newly arrived visitors normally suffer palpitations and altitude sickness. It is so empty and silent that it hardly seems to be part of the 20th century.

Titicaca, 195 km (120 miles) long and 100 km (62 miles) at its widest point, covers an area of 8,300 sq km (3,205 sq miles). It holds the record as the highest navigable lake in the world, 3,810 m (12,500 ft) above sea level, and the first steamer was put into service in 1862 after coming across the mountains in sections, loaded on the backs of llamas. Twenty-five rivers and streams feed Titicaca, the largest of them the Ramis, but there is only one small outlet, the Desaguadero, at the southern end. The average depth of the slightly brackish waters is 100 m (328 ft) but at the eastern end it reaches 180 m (590 ft). In the rainy season, between December and March, the water level varies by up to 5 m (16 ft) but most of the excess water evaporates in the sun and the wind, only 5 per cent of it escaping through the Desaguadero. Once the lake extended even further with Tiahuanaco, an important centre in about 600 BC, standing at the water's edge. Now the remnants of the city, with its glimpse of pre-Inca architecture, stand 32 km (20 miles) from the lake.

The surface temperature of the lake is around 14°C (57°F) but towards the bottom this drops to 12°C (54°F). Only two species of fish are native to Titicaca and this led to trout being introduced in the 1930s. The trout grew fat on the native fish and for years there was a thriving fish canning business in the area until eventually the waters were over-fished and the trout population was almost exhausted. Now fishing is forbidden in the hope that numbers will recover.

It may well have been the beauty of the lake, startling in its bleak situation, that led to the Inca myth that creation began here.

According to the legend, the greatest of the gods sent his children Manco Kapac and Mama Huaca to find an ideal place to found the dynasty of the Incas. They chose the Isla del Sol (the 'island of the sun') out in the lake and a sacred rock is said to mark the spot where the race began. Local Indians still venerate the island, together with its smaller sister, the Isla de la Luna (the 'island of the moon') which has the ruins of a temple dedicated to the Virgins of the Sun.

Several different groups of Indians live in the Titicaca region, and the isolation of the plateau over the centuries has made it possible for them to retain their strong cultural identity. There are the Altiplano Indians, whose bodies have adapted to the altitude in a remarkable way: medical studies have shown that they have extra red corpuscles and that their heart and lungs are larger than those of people living at lower altitudes. The Aymara Indians have lived on the shores since prehistoric times; they congregate to the south of the lake and have few ties with the Quechua Indians to the north, speaking a different language and adhering to their own customs. Taquile, one of Titicaca's 40 islands, is populated by Quechua-speaking Indians who make and sell colourful fabric in their own traditional designs. They grow barley and potatoes on steep Inca terraces climbing the hillside.

The Uros Indians originally took to living on floating islands in the lake as a way of cutting themselves off from the influences of the other groups. A few, perhaps 200–300, still live like this, building houses, churches and even schools on floating mats of torota, a reedy papyrus that grows in the marshy shallows. The top of the island is renewed with fresh layers of reeds as the water rots away the lower layers, but it is still possible for an unwary foot to go right through to the water beneath. Their distinctive boats are also made from totora, with several bundles lashed together to form the typical high prow and stern. It was the Egyptian style of these boats that prompted the explorer Thor Heyerdahl to cross the Atlantic in a reed boat, *Ra Two*, which he had made by skilled Titicaca boat builders, proving that the Egyptians might well have sailed to South America. Bundles of reeds set out to dry, and boats at various stages of construction, can usually be seen on the shores of the lake.

ANGEL FALLS

The highest waterfall in the world is one of the most recently discovered, and one of the most inaccessible, natural wonders of the world. Angel Falls, 15 times higher than Niagara, spurts from the side of a lofty mesa known as Auyán Tepui, or Devil Mountain, in the Guyana Highlands of eastern Venezuela. Here, in the dense jungle of the Gran Sabana, rise a series of huge tablelands or mesas, flat-topped and eroded into bizarre shapes, shot through with canyons, like the chasm into which Angel Falls cascades. A hundred years ago the area was unexplored and mysterious; fabulous tales about the region inspired Sir Arthur Conan Doyle's novel *The Lost World*, where travellers discovered a land where prehistoric creatures survived and man was an unwelcome intruder.

An American pilot, James Angel, was flying over the highlands in 1935, searching for gold. He had been shown a rich strike in a hidden river by an old prospector and had never again been able to locate the site, though he spent years searching. As he flew over Devil Mountain he spotted the falls and determined to return for a closer look. Two years later, with two companions, he attempted a landing on the top of mesa but the ground was neither as flat nor as firm as it looked and the plane crashed, sticking fast in a swamp. It took the three fliers 11 days to fight their way through the jungle, taking back to civilization stories of a mile-high waterfall. The plane was recovered only in 1970, and is on display in a museum at Ciudad Bolívar. It was not until 1949 that an American-led expedition managed to reach the foot of Angel Falls and make an accurate survey that established this as the world's highest waterfall. Jimmy Angel may never have found gold, but he found his place in history.

The Devil Mountain, like the rest of the South American mesas, was raised in the later Tertiary Period – the period that lasted from 65 million years ago to 2 million years ago. Erosion has hollowed out great pits and fissures on its flat top, capable of trapping large amounts of the Gran Sabana's tropical rainfall. The waters of Angel Falls leap out of the mesa some 61 m (200 ft) below the edge of the cliff above the Churún river. The full height is 980 m (3,215 ft); the first straight drop is 806 m (2,646 ft) and the remaining falls 172 m (564 ft). About 152 m (500 ft) wide at the base, the falls mask a huge natural amphitheatre. The great pool they create drains into the Churún, a tributary of the Caroní River.

Some way downstream is the red-brown Canaima lagoon, taking its colour from its high tannin content. Canaima is fed by seven waterfalls of its own and fringed with pink sand beaches. Rudy ('Jungle') Treffino and Charles Baugham founded a camp here in the 1950s, working with the friendly Camarata Indians, and called it by the Indian name for the goddess of the jungle. There are no foot trails to the base of the falls, but in the wet season, between June and September, it is possible to reach them by launch and canoe. During the remainder of the year the river is not deep enough for boats, so the falls can be viewed only from the sky, the way Jimmy Angel first saw them.

The largest of the mesas, the 2,810 m (9,219 ft) Mount Roraima, was first climbed in 1884 by two Englishmen who had trekked for eight weeks through the jungle to reach it, but it is now possible to reach Roraima by road and hike up to the cool, wet plateau, with its eroded lunar landscape. Rainfall here can be heavy and Roraima earns its Indian name meaning 'Mother of Streams'. Water flows down to feed rivers in three countries: the Orinoco in Venezuela, the Amazon in Brazil and the Essequiba in Guyana.

Few roads lead through Venezuela to the Guyana Plateau and the Gran Sabana and most are suitable only for four-wheel drive vehicles. The only substantial cities in this part of the country are Ciudad Bolívar and Ciudad Guayana, both situated on the Orinoco. Ciudad Bolívar was the city Simín Bolívar chose for his capital in 1817, the starting point for his famous campaign across the Andes in the fight for independence. Prospectors still gather here to sell their finds. Small towns in the area are inhabited entirely by diamond-hunters or those hopefully panning for gold along the rivers. Less romantic, but far more profitable, is the iron and steel industry of the fast-growing Ciudad Guayana, already Venezuela's fifth largest city. The government has plans for much expansion in the area, so in the future there could be more travellers to the 'Lost World'.

ANTARCTICA

THE ANTARCTIC PENINSULA

From the roughly circular continent of Antarctica, the long, curving finger of the mountainous peninsula reaches out 1,300 km (808 miles) towards Cape Horn at the southern tip of South America. Geologically, the mountains that divide it are part of the Andean chain, which became separated from South America some 28 million years ago. At the Vinson Massif, the mountains rise to Antarctica's highest peak, 5,140 m (16,363 ft) above sea level. When the first flights were made over the Antarctic in the 1920s, photographic evidence seemed to show that the Peninsula was really a string of islands separated by deep channels but this was disproved when the British Graham Land Expedition carried out a comprehensive survey of much of the Peninsula between 1934 and 1937.

The first ever sightings of Antarctica were made at the tip of the Antarctic Peninsula in the 1820s, though Captain James Cook, seeking the 'Terra Australis Incognita', the unknown southern continent of great riches rumoured since medieval times, must have come very near to finding it in the 18th century. Cook discovered South Georgia, naming the southern tip Cape Disappointment, when he relalized it was only an island and the endless packs of ice and freezing temperatures stopped him from proceeding further. He described the Antarctic lands as 'doomed by Nature to perpetual frigidness; never to feel the warmth of the sun's rays; whose horrible and savage aspect I have not words to describe'. Any lands further south would, he concluded, be even more horrifying. If any explorer travelled further, he said 'I shall not envy him the honour of the discovery; but I will be bold to say, that the world will not be benefited by it'.

The honour of sighting Antarctica for the first time is disputed. In 1820 Edward Bransfield, a British naval officer, was despatched to investigate the 'New South Shetland' islands, discovered the year before. He spent three months charting the area before bad weather forced him to sail due south. He found himself navigating a string of islands which 'formed a prospect the most gloomy that can be imagined, and the only cheer the sight afforded was that this might be the long sought southern continent, as land was undoubtedly seen in latitude 64°S'. The land sighted seems to have been the northern extremity of the Peninsula. However, some authorities favour the claims of the American sealer Nathaniel Palmer who sighted the coastline nine months later and described 'an extensive mountain country'. At the same time the Russian Captain Thaddeus von Bellingshausen was making an exploratory Antarctic voyage and he, too, probably sighted the mainland, though he made no claims. Both Palmer and Bellingshausen were halted by thick fog in the South Shetlands, and when the weather cleared found their ships anchored side by side.

The British named the Peninsula Graham Land after John Graham, who headed the British navy in Bransfield's time. The Americans called it Palmer Land and the Argentinians, their claim to the territory based on the age-link with South America, called it Tierra San Martin. It was only in 1964 that general agreement was reached to change the name to the Antarctic Peninsula. The first person to set foot on the Peninsula may have been the American sealer John Davies, who probably went ashore at Hughes Bay in 1821, but doubts have been cast on this landing because Davies was unsure whether he reached an island or the mainland itself. Other reports claim that the first footer was British naval officer John Biscoe in 1832.

The Norweigian whaler Captain C.A. Larsen explored both sides of the Peninsula in 1893–4 and discovered pieces of petrified wood, the first fossils found on the continent. Since then fossils of turtles, whales and penguins from 65 million years ago have been found as well as fossils of ferns and conifers from 250 million years ago, indicating a much warmer climate had once existed in this region.

THE ROSS ICE SHELF

In 1840 the British Captain James Clark Ross set out to locate the South Magnetic Pole. Ross had 17 years' experience in the Arctic and his ships, the 370 tonne *Erebus* and the 340 tonne *Terror*, were specially prepared for the southern ice, with double hulls and reinforced bulkheads. Courage and first-rate seamanship enabled him to penetrate the pack ice which had defeated previous explorers, and he managed to break through into open water in January 1841 only to find himself confronted by a perpendicular ice cliff of 'extraordinary appearance', rearing 60 m (200 ft) above the sea. 'What was beyond it we could not imagine', he wrote 'for being higher than our masthead, we could see nothing except the summit of a lofty range of mountains extending to the southward . . . we might with equal chance of success try to sail through the Cliffs of Dover, as penetrate such a mass.'

Ross sailed for 400 km (249 miles) along the foot of the lofty ice shelf which he called the Victoria Barrier, but was later named after him. The Ross Ice Shelf never fails to amaze travellers who come upon it for the first time. From a distance it looks like a long, white cliff, with Mount Erebus, at 4,075 m (13,370 ft) among the world's largest active volcanoes, rising behind it. Though it looks as solid as any coastline, the giant cliff is afloat. Close to, the desolate slab of ice is awe-inspiring, around 885 km (500 miles) wide and almost as long, its thickness ranging from 185 m (607 ft) to 760 m (2,494 ft). In places, the shelf is an unbroken line of cliffs; in others there are bays and headlands, like those of a regular coastline. The top is flat, and though the ice shelf is continuously melting below the waterline, fresh layers of snow turn to ice each year and reinforce its amazing bulk. Huge fissures can appear in the ice and sometimes these deepen until an iceberg breaks away. Icebergs often become moving mountains: in 1956 the icebreaker USS *Glacier* reported a berg 335 km (208 miles) long and 97 km (60 miles) wide.

The flat top of the ice shelf has made a useful base for several major Antarctic expeditions, the most famous of them being the race for the South Pole. In January 1911, the Norwegian party led by Roald Amundsen camped at the Bay of Whales on the Ross Ice Shelf. Most explorers would have been deterred from choosing such a base because of the danger of ice fractures, but Amundsen had studied the shelf carefully and decided that the Bay of Whales was more stable than most of the shelf. Before winter closed in, he was able to lay down a series of stores across the shelf ready for the journey the following season.

On 19 October Amundsen began his journey, taking a route along an unexplored glacier in the Queen Maud Range. The other contender in the race, Captain Robert Falcon Scott, set off on 1 November from his base on Ross Island, 97 km (60 miles) further from the Pole, taking a known route along the Beardmore Glacier. Scott's expedition was dogged by bad luck and bad judgement from the beginning, and when they finally reached the Pole on 17 January 1912, they found a Norwegian flag and Amundsen's tent. The Norwegians had reached the Pole just over a month before.

The way back was long, hungry and bitter. One of the party collapsed and died at the foot of the Beardmore Glacier. Captain 'Titus' Oates, knowing he could go no further, walked out into a blizzard. Scott and his two remaining companions pitched what was to be their last camp on the plateau of the ice shelf. Their bodies were found by a search party the following spring; a snow cairn was built above them, with a cross of skis.

THE WEDDELL SEA

The Weddell Sea, the large gulf that cuts into the continent east of the Antarctic Peninsula, extending 1,609 km (1,000 miles) across, takes its name from the British sealer Captain James Weddell, who sailed from the South Orkney Islands in 1823 determined to discover where the coast of the continent began. Other attempts to sail into the gulf, by the British ship *Williams* in 1820 and the Russian *Vostok* later the same year, were thwarted by impenetrable masses of ice. Weddell, in his brig *Jane*, was the first to penetrate further south than Cook, though the onset of winter forced him to turn back before he sighted land. He called the sea George, after King George IV, but in 1900 the name was changed to commemorate its discoverer.

It was to take many years to chart the coast of the Weddell Sea, for its huge bay is normally so choked with ice that it is hard to tell where water ends and land begins. The first successful attempt was made by the Scottish National Antarctic Expedition of 1902–4, under William S. Bruce in the *Scotia*; then the German South Polar Expedition of 1910–12 under Wilhelm Filchner explored the Luitpold Coast and discovered the ice shelf that bears his name.

In 1914 Ernest Shackleton, who had been a member of Scott's first expedition, planned a transpolar journey from the Weddell Sea to the Ross Sea. However, conditions in the Weddell Sea proved too much for him and his ship, the *Endurance*, became trapped in the pack ice. Shackleton and his crew were forced to abandon ship for the dubious safety of an ice floe and to watch the *Endurance* gradually being crushed. For five months they drifted towards the open sea. Shackleton said that they began to look on the floe as home and 'ceased to realize that it was but a sheet of ice floating on unfathomed seas'. As it began to crack and crumble, they were at last able to launch their small boats, rowing for a week before they reached Elephant Island. Most of the party camped under the boats while Shackleton and five companions made a heroic 1,287 km (800 mile) voyage to South Georgia for help. All 20 members of this expedition lived to tell the tale.

The Weddell Sea is still as merciless and terrifying as in Shackleton's time. As the Antarctic summer ends, new ice begins to form here up to two months ahead of the Ross Sea, on the far side of the continent. Strong currents moving clockwise churn the sea ice and, whipped by the wind, one floe piles upon another. The winter pack ice averages 2 m (6 ft) thick, but in places it reaches 4 m (13 ft). Much of it stays frozen all year and while most of the Antarctic sea ice is only one year old, some of the pack ice in the Weddell Sea is as much as seven years old.

Though the sea is such a forbidding place, there is life on and under its ice. One of Shackleton's companions was pursued by an aggressive leopard seal which had tracked him by following his shadow from under the ice floe. Leopard seals tend to live around the edges of the pack ice and prey on penguins and other seals. The crabeater seal is the most numerous of Antarctica's seals and can live to 40 years old. The Ross seal, often called the 'singing seal' because of its soft melodious 'cooing', is the rarest, with a population of something like 200,000. The Weddell seal is probably the hardiest, living under the ice in winter and gnawing breathing holes in the ice with its canine and incisor teeth. The under-ice lifestyle means that the young can be kept safe from predators but the constant gnawing means that the teeth become badly worn within ten years or so. Once they are no longer capable of making holes in the ice, the seals die, so few Weddells reach an age of more than twenty years.

Since man penetrated the Antarctic, 30 year-round scientific stations have been established on the continent and the work carried out here is of concern to every country in the world. In 1982 scientists at the Halley Station on the Weddell Sea began to suspect that the ozone layer, the region of the earth's stratosphere that acts as a filter and protects against the harmful effects of the sun, was depleted. By 1987 they found that in spring the ozone layer over the Antarctic was reduced to 40 per cent of the 1947 level and at one place to only 3 per cent. Since then, governments have been forced to agree on measures to reduce emissions of harmful chlorofluorocarbons, in the hope of limiting the damage.

AUSTRALASIA AND THE PACIFIC

Pancake Rocks, Punakaiki, South Island, New Zealand

AYERS ROCK

The majestic Ayers Rock, rising abruptly from the surrounding plain, is one of the peaks of an ancient, buried mountain range. It can be seen from 96 km (60 miles) away as a great purple mound but its amazing size – it is 384 m (1,260 ft) high, 2.5 km (1.5 miles) long and with a circumference of 9 km (5.5 miles) – is apparent only from a closer view. The rock is famed for its changing colours and moods as the sun moves across it, bright reds turning to deep pinks, then to brown and dark grey after sunset. In rain it takes on a silver hue as water cascades over surface ridges.

The Aborgines call the rock Uluru. For them it is a sacred site and every physical feature of the rock face has a special meaning from the Dreamtime, the time before time began, when the hero-ancestors and animal-men were creating the landscape. The earth-mother Bulari gave birth at the rock while on her travels and her cave is important in the rituals of local tribes. A double fold in the rock is the resting place of the lizard Kandju, who came here in search of a lost boomerang. The kangaroo-rat ancestors made the most easily ascendable slope with the angles of their tails hanging down to the ground; it is called Webo, 'the tail', and a chain has been installed to help modern climbers reach the top.

The Yankuntjatjara and the Pitjantjatjara are the tribes of the rock and their elders are guardians of the knowledge of the Dream-time trails that criss-cross the area. The nearer a man was born to the rock, the more influential he will be in local society. The important ceremonial sites of Uluru are out of bounds to Europeans but, though most visitors have only the haziest idea of its sacred connotations, most would admit that the rock projects a strong air of mystery.

Something like 200 mm (8 in) of rain falls on Ayers Rock every year and is caught by several waterholes. The most important of these is Magpie Springs (their local Aboriginal name is Mutitjilda), home of the sacred serpent of Uluru, who is said to ensure that there is always water by releasing it from his own body if necessary. At the foot of the rock, the water cascading off the sides has nurtured a

rich surround of grass and trees.

The first European to see the rock was the explorer Ernest Giles, who saw it from the north side of Lake Amadeus, 37 km (23 miles) to the north, in 1872. However, by the time he reached it the following year, a second explorer, William Gosse, had found the rock and named it after Sir Henry Ayers, the Premier of South Australia.

Giles wrote of his first impressins: 'Its appearance and outline is most imposing, for it is simply a mammoth monolith that rises out of the sandy desert soil around, and stands with a perpendicular and totally inaccessible face at all points, except one slope near the north-west end, and that at least is but a precarious climbing ground . . .'

Since then, the idea of scaling the monolith has caught the imagination of many visitors. Some have not lived to tell the tale: there have been several fatal falls and even more heart attacks. The victims are remembered on small plaques at the base of Ayers Rock, including the schoolboy from Carey Baptist Grammar School who fell, and the Melbourne man whose 'lifelong ambition' was to climb Ayers Rock but who suffered a heart attack during the ascent.

Another tragedy at Ayers Rock hit the headlines worldwide in 1980 when Mrs Lindy Chamberlain claimed that a dingo had made off with her baby daughter Azaria, snatching her from a tent where she was sleeping with her brother. The child's body was never found and after a furore of publicity Lindy Chamberlain was found guilty of murdering the baby and sent to prison. When more evidence came to light, a miscarriage of justice was declared and she was released. Dingos certainly prowl the area and have been known to attack, but foreign press reports missed the strange echoes of Aboriginal myth which believes in a devil-dingo once sent to punish the people of Uluru for their wrong-doing.

Thirty two km (20 miles) to the west is a collection of rocks called the Olgas. The highest of them at 546 m (1,791 ft) is taller than Ayers Rock. Giles, who found the Olgas 'wonderful and grotesque', named them after the Grand Duchess of Russia who married the King of Spain. The Aborigines call it Katatjuta, the 'place of many heads', as the rocks were believed to be the petrified remains of giants who lived here during the Dreamtime.

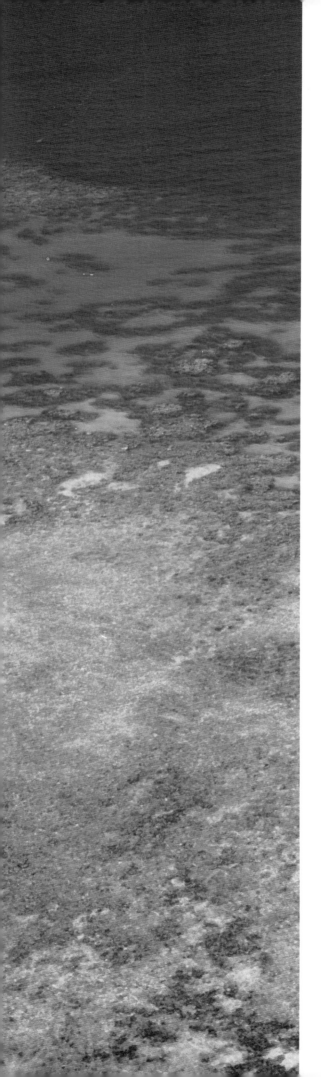

GREAT BARRIER REEF

The immense undersea world of the Great Barrier Reef is an extravagantly beautiful labyrinth of over 2,000 reefs, cays, rocky islands and lagoons extending more than 2,000 km (1,250 miles) along Australia's east coast from the Torres Strait at the northern tip of the continent to just south of the Tropic of Capricorn. Lying on the shallow continental shelf off Queensland, the Great Barrier Reef stretches out to sea for up to 330 km (200 miles) to the line where the shelf gives way to the depths of the Pacific Ocean.

Something like a third of the area is taken up by separate reefs, too numerous to be counted, some of them only a couple of metres (yards) across. Others have an area as large as 50 sq km (19 sq miles). They may poke their heads above water or nestle well beneath the surface. Small cays built up from accumulated sand and coral debris rise above the reef and vegetation takes root from seeds carried by wind or birds.

The coral (*see inset*) is built up by millions upon millions of marine polyps, tiny primitive creatures, which develop hard skeletons by secreting lime. The skeletons are left behind when the creatures die and new generations build on them, forming ever-growing gardens of delicate branches, lacy fans and nobbly clusters. The skeletons are white, but the more than 300 species of living corals give a vivid range of pinks, blues, mauves and yellows to the reef. One of the most extraordinary of the reef sights follows a full moon in late spring each year, when many thousands of corals all spawn simultaneously and millions of tiny sperm and eggs cloud the water.

Pacific breakers constantly pound the outer line of the reef. In the wet season, between November and February, heavy rains beat down. An occasional cyclone can whip up waves powerful enough to uproot sections of reef from the sea bed and wash away some of the smaller coral islands. The Great Barrier Reef stands up to all this weathering because it is a living entity, constantly renewing itself. Drilling on the reef has proved that the coral can be as much as 500 m (1,640 ft) thick. However, coral can grow only in shallow water, up to 50 m (164 ft) deep, because this is as far as the sun can penetrate, and the temperature must be at 20°C (68°F) all the year round. It also needs salt water; it ends at Papua New Guinea because of the huge influx of fresh water from the Fly River into the Gulf of Papua.

The ever-growing world of the coral provides a home for an enormously diverse and rich marine life; sponges, anemones, sea urchins and starfish, clams, crabs, oysters, lobsters and shrimps, mussels, worms, flagtails and snappers. In all, there are more than 1,300 species of fish and 4,000 or more species of mollusc, all adding extra colour to the reef. Sea cows are found here and humpback whales arrive from Antarctica every winter. Sharks have never caused problems around the reef; more dangerous to the unwary visitor are the stone fish that sit on the bottom, their camouflage so perfect that they cannot be distinguished from the stones around them, and the poisonous scorpion fish. Between the end of October and the beginning of February, turtles crawl up the beaches to lay their eggs and the young hatch out between mid-January and April.

Until recent times, the inaccessibility of the Great Barrier Reef was its protection. Now the pressurees of modern development are encroaching, with some of the coral islands being mined for limestone fertilizer, and drilling for oil and minerals is well under way. However, the main threat to the reef in the past 30 years has been the appearance of hordes of voracious crown-of-thorns starfish which consumed large portions of the reef in the late 1960s and 1970s. Since then the numbers of hungry starfish have diminished, allowing the reef to renew itself. Experts say that they have evidence of similar attacks in the past and that the explosion in numbers is a cyclical occurrence.

The reef is Queensland's major tourist attraction, with opportunities to explore ranging from snorkelling to glass-bottom boats or marine observatories, where it is possible to descend to the reef and view all its wonders in dry comfort. Most of the resort islands scattered along the coast are not true coral islands but are the tops of mountains flooded at the end of the last Ice Age. Though they are fringed by reefs, they are not part of the Great Barrier Reef itself. Of the genuine coral cay islands, Heron Island is a bird-lovers' haven in the middle of the outer reef, Lady Elliot Island is on the reef's southernmost tip and Lady Musgrave Island is an uninhabited national park.

THE VICTORIA COAST

The westernmost coast of Victoria was once a fearful place, one of the wildest seascapes of Australia, where rocks and the fierce surf battering the shore were a byword amongst mariners. Now the dangers are known and charted and ships no longer founder here, but along the 30 km (19 mile) length of Point Campbell National Park the ocean is still carving grottos, arches and pillars out of the cliffside and the scene changes from year to year.

The cliffs were once part of the seabed, a thick layer of shells, mud and limestone, built up some 25 million years ago when the sea level was 100 m (330 ft) higher than today. When the sea dropped, these calcified deposits formed the coastline. Over time, the constant bombardment of waves and the pebbles carried by them eats into the rocks, forcing them apart and carrying off the softer layers. The towering stone stacks called the 12 Apostles (*see right, inset*) were originally part of the mainland but are now cut off by the pounding waves. In spite of the name, there are no longer 12; several have disappeared beneath the water and it is only a matter of time before the rest follow. Further west, at the Blowhole, the sea has burrowed its way several metres (yards) into the cliff, filling the air with its thundering and snorting. In only a few decades, the sea has hollowed out the archway known as London Bridge (*see right*) but it is constantly worrying and weakening its supports, so that eventually the 'bridge' will be turned into a new row of 'apostles'.

The Great Ocean Road hugs the coast for most of its 320 km (199 mile) length, leaving it only to climb over the forest-clad Cape Otway, where the gullies are lined with ferns rising to 5 m (16 ft) or more. Once, many enormous trees grew here; Melba Gully nature reserve contains one of the few remaining giant gums, its trunk 25 m (82 ft) in circumference.

The 120 km (75 miles) of shoreline from Cape Otway to Port Fairy has earned its nickname of 'the Shipwreck Coast' with more than 80 major shipping disasters. The most famous is the tragic wreck of the *Loch Ard*, an iron-hulled clipper that ran on to the reef of an offshore island in 1878 and went down within 120 m (390 ft) of the coast. Of the 54 passengers and crew aboard, only two survived: an 18-year old apprentice, Thomas Pearce, who was washed into a narrow gorge, and a young girl, Eva Carmichael, who clung to a spar that caught fast on the rocks. Though injured, Pearce swam to rescue her and they spent the night in a cave that can still be seen in the cliffside. Rescue came next morning and Pearce was awarded a gold medal for valour. The deep gorge in the cliff still bears the name of the ill-fated ship and on the hillside are graves of the victims, whole families among them.

Flagstaff Hill Maritime Village preserves relics of the *Loch Ard* and a number of other wrecks: the *Newfield*, which lost eight men when it ran on to the rocks while carrying a cargo of rock salt from Brisbane; the *Falls of Halladale*, which remained stuck fast on the reef with all sails set for two months in 1908; and *La Bella*, sunk in 1905 on the last leg of her voyage to New Zealand. Seven men drowned as she went down, while the people of the nearby town watched helplessly. The wreck was discovered by accident only in 1982 by a diver hunting fish. It had been carried 400 m (1,300 ft) from the site of the shipwreck.

The Victoria coast has proved more hospitable to the southern right whales than to 19th-century shipping, and at Logan's Beach, Warrnambool, there is a viewing area for the 'whale nursery'. Right whales got their name from the early European whalers, simply because they were the right whales to catch. They were easy to hunt because they moved slowly and were rich in oil and bone. Though they spend all summer in sub-antarctic waters, in winter they gather round the coasts of Australia, South Africa and South America to calve. These whales are barrel-shaped and unaggressive, weighing an average of 55 tonnes and measuring 14 to 18 m (45 to 60 ft). Their large heads are one third the length of the whole body and they display varying patterns of horny growths called callosities. The calves weight 4 to 5 tonnes at birth. They are extremely boisterous and playful and watching the whales 'breaching' – diving first, breaking the surface and hurling themselves high into the air, then landing with a tremendous splash – is one of the most memorable sights of this part of Australia.

WAVE ROCK

Wave Rock towers 15 m (49 ft) over the Australian plain that surrounds it, a huge granite breaker that seems just about to crash over the dry ground. Minerals and chemical deposits have been washed down the wave by rainwater, streaking the whole of its 100 m (328 ft) length with reddish-brown, black, yellow and grey, completing the effect of the rolling ocean. As the water evaporates, leaving behind the chemical deposits – carbonates and iron hydroxide – the colours continue to deepen. The rock can be seen to best effect in the morning, when direct sunlight brings out the depth and brilliance of the colours.

The wave does not stand alone; it is an overhanging rock on the northern end of an enormous outcrop known as Hyden Rock. The wave itself is large enough to contain a dam, built in 1928 as a badly-needed watering place for the horses of the settlers. Once, probably around 2,700 million years ago, this was a vertical cliff face, but the forces of erosion have scooped it out, leaving the curling, wave-like outline. At one time scientists believed that the sculpture was created by the wind, carrying sand dust particles along with it and whittling away at the rock. However, current theory asserts that the wind is not capable of sufficient abrasion to create rock formations and that its action is limited to modifying, polishing and shaping. Geologists think that Hyden Rock was once partially buried. Water seeping through the ground combined with decaying organic matter to form mild acids which gradually ate away the underside of the rock. Later, the surrounding soil was washed away to reveal the cliff's hollowed profile, and the wind continued the sculpting work.

The wave is the most beautiful of a number of interesting formations in the area. A trail along the base of the rock leads through native bush to the Hippo's Yawn, a rock hollowed out like a monster animal's yawning mouth, probably formed in the same way as the wave. A few kilometres (miles) to the north is a set of nobbly outcrops known as the Humps, and nearby is Bates Cave with well-preserved examples of Aboriginal art in the form of hand paintings. Alongside are ancient *gnamma* holes, where the Aborigines exploited cracks in the bedrock to bore for water.

According to legend, Bates Cave was the home of the dreaded 'Mulka the Terrible'. He was the result of a forbidden love affair between an Aboriginal girl and a young man from an enemy tribe; he had crossed eyes, which were the marks of the devil. As an adult, more than 2.7 m (9 ft) tall, he terrorized the whole area with his indiscriminate killings, dragging off the bodies of his victims to eat them at leisure in his cave. When his mother found him eating a dead child and berated him, he murdered her too. At last the local tribes came together to hound him from his cave.

The town of Hyden stands on the very edge of the grain belt that stretches for millions of hectares (acres) across Western Australia. This region produces one fifth of the wheat, over one third of the oats and nearly a quarter of the barley grown in the state. Beside its crops and its famous rock formations the area is known for another natural wonder: gold. The first strike was at Southern Cross to the north of Hyden in 1887, but the gold soon gave out and by 1892 the gold rush had moved to Coolgardie and Kalgoorlie. In the boom years hundreds of thousands of hopeful prospectors flocked to the area, and in Kalgoorlie alone 100 mines worked simultaneously. Within 10 years the population of the towns had shrunk back to a few thousand, though the imposing buildings and wide main streets echo the prosperity of the boom time. Gold mining still continues in the region, a recent strike at Boddington leading to the opening of two new mines.

THE PINNACLES

Dutch sailors, 300 years ago, noted the sand-dune desert that is now Nambung National Park, Western Australia, and recorded it on their navigational maps. At the time, they assumed that the pinnacles, the spires and sturdy blocks they saw rising out of the sand, were the remains of long-abandoned and ruined cities. However, the slopes they saw were made of limestone, a natural phenomenon unshaped by man. Thousands upon thousands of them cluster on the desert floor in a wide variety of shapes and sizes: some rise to sharp points, some have blunt or rounded tops, others are sculpted columns. The largest are 5 m (16 ft) high and measure up to 2 m (7 feet) around the base.

It was once thought that the Pinnacles were the petrified remains of ancient woodlands but it is now generally agreed that this incredible landscape was formed entirely from sand washed ashore tens of thousands of years ago, then blown into steep rolling hills by the wind and stabilized by vegetation. In the wet season, rainwater seeped into the sand, dissolving the calcium carbonate within it. The summer heat then dried the calcium carbonate so that it cemented sand grains together deep within the dunes. Over many thousands of years this formed into soft limestone. If the process continues for long enough, a much harder type of limestone is produced. In the area of the Pinnacles this happened only near the surface of the dunes where water penetration was great enough to allow a layer of harder 'caprock' to form. The remains of this layer can be seen in the mushroom-like 'hats' sitting on top of some of the Pinnacles.

Any cracks in the hard top layer meant that plant roots could reach down into the soft limestone below in search of water. As the roots rotted away, they left behind channels which allowed water to move freely and nibble away at the limestone, gradually sculpting the shapes of the Pinnacles, though they were still completely carved by sand. The capstone layer eroded less easily than the soft base, whence the larger stone top on a slender base. Over the past 25,000 years the climate changed, becoming much drier and leading to movement among the sands. New sand covered and killed vegetation, destabilizing the dunes. First the layer of sand cover

blew away, then the sand that had filled the channels between the eroded pillars of limestone disappeared, and eventually the Pinnacles were exposed, ready to be turned into even more fantastic shapes by weathering.

Within the park can be seen all the stages of pinnacle formation, from indented limestone cliffs showing the early stages of water penetration, through rock towers still half embedded in sand, to the isolated pinnacles standing tall above the desert. The process continues all the time and some pinnacles have already toppled after their bases had become too fragile to support their weight.

Amongst the Pinnacles are scattered hundreds of pencil-sized formations like small twigs. These are brittle, fossilized plant roots called rhizoliths left from the time of the stabilized dunes. Other interesting fossils found in the ancient dune area look like eggs but are actually the pupal cases of the weevil heptopius, often still showing the hole in one end whence the weevil emerged.

Aborigines lived amid the Pinnacles 6,000 years ago and many artifacts from that period have been found and identified. However, there is no evidence of more modern Aboriginal occupation and this leads experts to believe that the Pinnacles were exposed at that time, then covered again by sand and in due course laid bare again at some time within the last few hundred years. The discovery of several ancient artifacts cemented to the pillars by the same process that formed the limestone in the first place, lends weight to the theory that the Pinnacles have been exposed more than once. Eventually sand may cover them again. If not, erosion will eat them away, though they will probably stand for thousands of years.

Four different dune systems are to be found in the complex dune country that makes up Nambung National Park surrounding the Pinnacles. The foredune system borders the ocean, with dense low grasses. Behind these comes steep, light-coloured dunes, the quindalup system. New sand often alights on them from the beach area and they are covered with coastal scrub, including various species of acacia. Further back from the sea are the older, brownish sands of the spearwood system, often covering limestone, and supporting low woodland and heath, dotted with bright orange banksia flowers. Bird watchers can find seldom-seen species here. The oldest of the dune systems is the bassendean, which occurs on the eastern side of Nambung, its sands rich in silica and its vegetation consisting of wood shrubs and low woodlands.

BUNGLE BUNGLE

The Bungle Bungles existed 350 million years ago, yet it was only in 1982 that they were announced to the Australian public as a rediscovered 'lost world'. Until then, the strange, high-coloured range in a remote corner of the Kimberley Plateau region of Western Australia was known only to the locals. Though the main route from Perth to Darwin passed within 30 km (19 miles) of the Bungle Bungles, no tourists thought to turn off the road to visit them.

Their anonymity came to an end when a television producer, filming in the Kimberley region for the first programme in the series 'The Wonder of Western Australia', heard mention of the Bungle Bungles and decided to investigate. He was so impressed by the great expanse of tightly packed beehive-shaped rocks with their black and orange stripes that they not only took up most of his second and third programme but also took fast hold on the imagination of television viewers.

The first modern-day explorers who attempted to penetrate the range found it a difficult, inhospitable place, full of giant ravines, precipitous slopes and treacherous rock that could crumble away at a touch. Daytime temperatures often reach 50°C (122°F) and the heavy rainfalls between December and March set rivers raging and cause flash floods that make the gorges impassable.

The fascinating, forbidding range carries signs of Aboriginal habitation from ancient times in carvings on the rock faces. The early ancestors of today's Aborigines arrived in Australia some 40,000 years ago and reached the Kimberley region not long after-wards. For many centuries they held undisputed rights over the land and developed a strong relationship with the harsh, unyielding desert terrain.

Once the European colonizers arrived, the traditional way of life of the Aborigines was under threat; from 1788, when the first governor, Captain Arthur Phillip, arrived from England, all land in Australia was considered to be the property of the crown. The Aborigines, with no community structure capable of challenging the colonial incursers, gradually became dispossessed. It was some time before the Aborigines of the Kimberley region felt the effects of the new order, but by the beginning of the 20th century the best of the land in the area was being settled on pastoral leases. As skirmishes broke out between the traditional inhabitants and the

newcomers, the Aborigines used the Bungle Bungles as a hiding place. Whenever they were pursued by angry settlers, they took refuge in the striped beehive ranges, using notched trees as ladders, then pulling them up behind them so that it was impossible for their enemies to follow.

Years of heavy cattle grazing in the area damaged the land irreparably. As vegetation was trampled or uprooted, the soil was destabilized and the top layer washed away in summer storms. Water holes dried up and plants, which that had always provided food for the Aborigines living a simple existence on the land, disappeared for ever. The Bungle Bungles were left to slumber until television announced their existence.

The range, fascinating and forbidding at the same time, is part of a 200 m (650 ft) high sandstone plateau, long ago part of the ocean floor. Fish once swam over the rocks, but few creatures, beyond snakes, frogs and lizards, live here now. However, a few of the deep gorges shelter a rich plant life of trees and creepers. Here the unique Bungle Bungle fan palm, a slender tree with a crown of spreading leaves, has its roots anchored in the near-vertical cliffs.

In spite of its rugged appearance, this is a fragile landscape. The sandstone is soft and it is only the skin formed by silica and algae –

the horizontal bands of black and orange – that protect it. If this is damaged, the rock soon breaks up and, when the rains come, washes away. Once the Bungle Bungles had become famous, it was obvious that the land would need protection. By 1984, scenic flights had started and bush-walkers were exploring the ranges. The government thought hard about the problems of taking over the area as a national park, as they calculated that it would cost three times as much as a park in a more populous part of the country. However, they decided that there was no alternative and the 7,770 sq km (3,000 sq miles) Bungle Bungle National Park was proclaimed in 1987.

The Kimberley region is still considered one of Australia's last frontiers, a land of pioneers. Far more accessible than the Bungle Bungles but still comparatively little visited are Windjana and Geikie Gorges, both national parks, where the limestone cliffs are 350 million years old, part of fossilized coral reefs that are among the best preserved in the world. The Fitzroy River flows through Geikie, crocodiles basking on its banks; at Windjana the river runs only in the rainy season.

ROTORUA

The local nickname for Rotorua, in New Zealand's North Island, is 'Sulphur City' and there is always a pungent smell in the air. It stands at the centre of an area of seething geothermal activity: hot springs, geysers, hissing steam vents and amazing mud lakes where the sludgy contents rise in great glupping bubbles that burst violently enough to splatter the banks.

Just south of the town is Whakarewarewa, the 'place of the rising steam'. It is aptly named, for the country's largest geyser erupts regularly here. Its display is heralded by a plume of three jets from a smaller geyser called the Prince of Wales Feathers, which plays for several hours. Then Pohutu, the 'splashing water' suddenly shoots upwards, sometimes reaching 30 m (100 ft) and playing for up to 40 minutes at a time.

In Victorian times, the fan-like pink and white silica terraces on the shores of Lake Rotomahana were the chief attraction of the area, but these were destroyed in the eruption of Mount Tarawera in 1886. As the mountain split in two, the noise of the explosion could be heard 160 km (1,000 miles) away. Flames shot 300 m (1,000 ft) into the air and rocks, fireballs and mud rained down. The land tilted violently, and the terraces disappeared for ever.

Following the explosion, a new set of wonders came into being. In Waimangu thermal valley, a vivid emerald-green pool fills the 40 m (131 ft) explosion pit, the most southerly crater of Mount Tarawera's eruption. Waimangu Cauldron is a hot lake (temperature 50°C, 122°F), covering 5 ha (12 acres) and above it the Cathedral Rocks (*see inset*) steam constantly. The shores of Rotomahana now have another attraction, the Warbrick Terrace. Algae and mineral deposits in the water flowing down from the topmost platform colour the terrace in greens, oranges, browns and blacks. The geyser that gave the valley its name, which means 'black water', was once the largest in the world. At its most active, between 1901 and 1904, its muddy coloured waters rose as high as 500 m (1,600 ft).

The Maori village of Te Wairoa, completely buried by the 1886 eruption, has been excavated from its covering of mud and ash revealing, among other buildings, the blacksmith's shop complete with bellows, anvil and tools, the remains of the flour mill, and the hotel, where an English tourist was among those who died.

The most colourful of the thermal areas is Waiotapu (*see right*), where the Rainbow Crater, the Devil's Ink-pots and the Artist's Palette are coloured by various natural chemical elements. Sulphur streaks the rocks with yellow, orange comes from antimony, red from iron oxide, green from arsenic and black from carbon and sulphur. Waiotapu has the largest terraces in the area, built up from deposits of silicate of lime left as overflow water from the enormous Champagne Pool evaporates. Violent explosions more than 800 years ago have left craters up to 20 m (66 ft) in diameter and 12 m (39 ft) deep. In some, boiling springs bubble, while others are decorated with delicate sulphur crystal formations.

George Bernard Shaw was both fascinated and appalled by Hell's Gate at Tikitere and said he wished that he had never seen the place; he claimed it was too much like Hades. Tikitere is a contraction of a Maori phrase meaning 'there floats my precious one', reflecting the legend of a Maori princess, Huritini, who committed suicide by throwing herself into the boiling pool. Hell's Gate boasts the only hot waterfall in the southern hemisphere with a temperature of 38°C (100°F), fed by hot lakes above.

Since the 1870s, visitors have come to Rotorua to relax in the thermal springs, said to be especially good for treating rheumatism and arthritis, and most of the plentiful motels have their own baths. This free use of the water may be one of the reasons why some of the thermal areas no longer perform as dramatically as is the past.

MOUNT RUAPEHU

Mount Ruapehu, the highest point of the central volcanic plateau of New Zealand's North Island at 2,797 m (9,175 ft), wears a year-round cap of snow. Its truncated cone holds a steaming hot lake of green, acidic water surrounded by snowy precipices. Most of the time it is deceptively calm but the name Ruapehu means 'exploding lake' and it is still capable of sudden violence. Back in 1945 clouds of ash settled over a radius of 80 km (50 miles). In the eruptions of 1969 and 1975 sulphurous water and mud showered the upper slopes and in 1988 the crater spat hot rock.

In 1953 Ruapehu brought tragedy when Crater Lake overflowed, sending a violent surge of water down the Whangaehu River and carrying a great weight of stones and boulders along with it. The powerful flood demolished a railway bridge 35 km (22 miles) away, just before the Wellington to Auckland express was due to cross it. The train had no time to stop and the engine and five carriages crashed into the swollen river, killing over 150 people.

With its two sister volcanoes, Mount Ruapehu is part of Tongariro National Park. Mount Tongariro, 1,968 m (6,458 ft), is the oldest and quietest of the three. Mount Ngauruhoe, 2,291 m (7,515 ft), is the youngest (formed in the last 2,500 years) and the most active. Its perfectly symmetrical cone frequently puffs smoke, leaving a coating of ash across the snow, and as recently as 1954–5 it was in more or less constant eruption for nine months.

The name Tongariro is deeply rooted in Maori legend, which relates that the mountains of North Island were once gathered together in this central area. Trouble came when they fought for the favours of the graceful Pihanga, the mountain on the southern shore of Lake Taupo. The victor was Tongariro, who chased off his rivals. Taranaki went west until he was stopped by the sea and took root as Mount Egmont; the mist that gathers on the summit is caused by his sad tears. Putauaki, now Mount Edgecumbe, made his home to the north of the Kaingaroa Plain.

The fires of the mountains came later. The revered priest Ngatorairangi was exploring Tongariro when he became trapped by a snowstorm and was in danger of freezing to death. He prayed for help from his priestess sisters in his Polynesian homeland and they

sent the fire demons to shoot flames from the mountain tops, warning and reviving Ngatorairangi. Giving thanks, he hurled the body of his slave girl into the pit of Ngaurhoe, which the Maoris still call by her name, Auruhoe. He left behind the name Tongariro, 'carried by the south wind' as a reminder of his successful prayer.

Mount Ruapehu offers the best skiing in New Zealand and the Whakapapa ski fields, on the western slopes, have been popular since 1913. The road runs 1,524 m (5,000 ft) to the 'Top O' the Bruce', where chairlifts take over. Though Whakapapa means 'laid out flat' this does not refer to the ski slopes but to an ancient battle, when the corpses of the vanquished were laid in rows on the mountain top. The Turoa ski field on the south-west slopes above the town of Okahune was opened in 1979 and offers wide slopes with runs up to 4 km (2.5 miles) long, and the less accessible Tukino fields on the windswept eastern side have a wilder, more adventurous atmosphere.

A circular track, which takes six or seven days to walk and is suitable only for the fittest, runs round the three volcanoes. A less demanding track leads to the Ketetahi Springs on the northern side of Mount Ruapehu, where hot streams bubble from the hillside, blowholes roar throatily and miniature geysers spurt constantly. Above, the path leads on to the middle crater of Tongariro, which still grumbles quietly. Here, there are deep blue and emerald green lakes and an exciting view far over the smoking volcanoes. Other beauties of the mountainside include the Silica Springs, running over rocks coloured by minerals borne by the water, the Taranaki Falls, shooting 21 m (70 ft) over an old lava flow, and the Whakapapanui stream which flows through rich beech forests. On the eastern flank of the volcanoes is the wilderness of the Rangipo Desert, not a real desert but a desolate, exposed area where nothing grows.

Below the mountains, to the north of Lake Rotoaira, are the restored earthworks of Te Porere, the site of a pitched battle in the Maori wars of 1860–70. It was the chief of one of the tribes that fought in the battle who gave the three mountains to the New Zealand government in 1886. He considered the land sacred and was determined to prevent it being divided, so he offered it for use as a national park.

WAITOMO CAVE

The northern King Country, in New Zealand's North Island, is gently undulating, lush green countryside but the limestone beneath the surface is riddled with caverns, potholes and underground streams. Waitomo is like many other karst areas in the world, except for the fantasy subterranean world of the Glow-Worm Grotto, where thousands of tiny creatures shine like a forest of miniature fairy-lights.

The entrance is an opening in the hillside about 18 m (59 ft) above the spot where the river flows down into the caves. Sparkling stalactites and stalagmites decorate the galleries and grottos, but they are just a prelude to the main attraction. Where the cave path meets a large underground lake, over-arched by limestone vaulting, visitors take to boats that slide off silently as the electric lights go out.

At first the darkness seems complete, then pinpricks of greenish-blue light begin to appear near the roof of the cave, 15 m (50 ft) above, more and more of them every second. Though each individual light is minute, as a body they unite to light the cavern with a strange, unearthly glow. It becomes light enough to read the time by a wristwatch. The cave has transformed itself into a natural planetarium, with a whole galaxy of stars twinkling above. Curtains of cobwebby filaments shimmer in the light.

The New Zealand glow-worm is unlike the species of glow-worm found in other countries, which light up as a prelude to mating. These glow-worms are the larvae of a type of gnat, *Arachnocampa luminosa*, that flourishes in dark, damp habitats and light up to attract their food. The larvae, their rear ends luminescent, sit inside a hammock of threads attached to the cave roof, and extrude filaments that glitter with scores of sticky droplets. Midges breeding on the water below are attracted by the light and become ensnared in the sticky threads. The glow-worms then have a ready storehouse of food and can haul in their lines and feed on their victims at lesiure.

The glow-worm spends about nine months in the larval stage, and during this time it often catches and eats the adult of the species, as an addition to its diet. In spite of this cannibalistic behaviour the *Arachnocampa luminosa* is a sensitive creature and any light or noise will cause it to extinguish its glow immediately. Eventually it will spend a couple of weeks in a cocoon stage, then the adult emerges and within just a few days it will have mated, laid its eggs and died.

The other important caves in the Waitomo complex are the Aranui and the Ruakuri. In the Aranui, thousands of little hollow straw-like stalactites hang in delicate clusters from the ceiling. The river does not penetrate the Aranui but it does run right through the Ruakuri. This cave used to attract its share of visitors but it has been closed to the public until a long-running dispute over Maori ownership of the land has been settled. The only way to view Ruakuri now is on a 'black water rafting' trip. These adventurous expeditions have become extremely popular since their introduction in the late 1980s. The 'rafts' are rubber inner tubes, and the rafters are equipped with wetsuits and cavers' helmets, complete with headlamps. The tubes drift along the underground stream, through passages dotted with bright glow-worms and decorated with weird rock formations and stalactites, down miniature waterfalls and sometimes through cuttings so narrow that rafters have to scramble over the rocks, pulling their inner tubes behind them.

It was the Maoris who named the caves Waitomo, meaning 'water-going-in', because of the underground river that links the system, but the belief that the caves were the home of fierce dragons was strong enough to make them declare the area taboo and stay well away. Waitomo became more widely known only in the last century when a New Zealander, Fred Mace, navigated the river on a raft woven from the leaves and stems of flax.

MILFORD SOUND

Maoris call Milford Sound Piopiotahi, 'the solitary thrush', telling the story of the discoverer Maui who went in search of immortality for mankind, taking the bird with him. However, the song of the thrush woke the goddess of death, Hinenui-te-po, who crushed Maui to death, killing mankind's hopes of everlasting life along with him. The thrush flew to this remote New Zealand fiord to spend the rest of its life mourning.

Milford Sound (*see right*) is the jewel of Fiordland National Park, on the south-west coast of South Island. Along with more than a dozen other fiords, it was created when retreating glaciers left deeply indented valleys, drowned by the incoming sea. This long finger of ocean reaches inland for 20 km (12 miles). Vast cliffs rise majestically from deep bottle-green water while waterfalls plunge from hanging valleys, formed when smaller glaciers receded and disappeared. One of the most picturesque is Bowen Falls, which plunges down 162 m (531 ft) in two tiers. Mitre Peak, looming dramatically 1,695 m (5,560 ft) on the south side, dominates the Sound. The British author Rudyard Kipling, overcome by the grandeur of the scene, called it 'the eighth wonder of the world'.

Up to a century ago, most of Fiordland was inaccessible, though Maoris had long made forays to collect the pale greenstone known as tangiwai or 'grieving waters'. Captain James Cook recorded the area on maps in 1770, when he sailed into the largest of the fiords as darkness fell and called it Dusky Bay, now Dusky Sound. In 1773 he spent more than a month there, exploring further and experimenting with brewing spruce beer to cure scurvy. As the news of his findings spread, sealers and whalers moved in, hunting their quarry almost to extinction. By the 1880s, gold prospectors were making their way to Fiordland, their journey made easier with the discovery, by explorer Quinton MacKinnon, of the mountain pass between Lake Te Anau and Milford 1887. The road which now leads to the Sound became possible only with the completion of the Homer Tunnel through the cliffside in 1953.

Milford Track, the 53 km (33 mile) four-day hike from Lake Te Anau in the south-east, has long borne the reputation of being the 'finest walk in the world'. Hikers follow in the footsteps of the early pioneers as the track winds through rainforests where beech trees are clothed in green moss, through gardens of gigantic ferns, alongside rippling streams full of trout and over the 1,073 m (3,520 ft) pass named after MacKinnon. The walls of the mountains are laced by waterfalls. One, fed by a creek that leaps over the cliff top, has created the peaceful Hidden Lake; another is the 630 m (2,067 ft) Sutherland Falls (*see inset*), named after the hermit Donald Sutherland who lived a solitary life at Milford Sound for years. The rainfall here is prodigious, more than 6 m (20 ft) a year, and after a storm countless cascades tumble from the cliffs until the whole world seems full of the sound of rushing water. Fiordland has proved a refuge for more than one rare species of bird. Both the kakapo, a flightless parrot that burrows underground, and the blue-green takahe, with its scarlet feet and bill, are found here. The takahe had been presumed extinct until a flourishing colony was discovered at Milford Sound in the 1940s.

Less welcome creatures of the area are the tiny black sandflies that rise in clouds and bite like mosquitoes. They plagued Captain Cook, who wrote that they were 'most mischievous animals – small black flies, which are very numerous and so troublesome that they exceed everything of the kind I have ever met with'. According to legend, it was the dreaded Hinenui-te-po who sent the sandflies and bade them multiply. The gods who created the fiords were so delighted with their work that they could only sit and gaze, so the sandflies were dispatched to spur them into action.

THE VOLCANOES OF HAWAII

Hawaiians believe that Pele, the fire goddess, the creator of mountains and burner of forests, has made her home deep within the island volcanoes. Legend says that she came here in ancient times, fleeing from her angry sister, the sea goddess. Pele had already tried to make her home on several other islands but each time she was discovered and driven out. Finally, she found a safe haven, deep within the volcanic mountain of Hawaii's Big Island. Local people have learned to live with her unpredictable nature and sudden tempers in one of the world's most active and thrilling volcanic areas.

The volcanoes Mauna Loa and Kilauea are linked directly to the magma, or molten rock, below the Pacific Plate on which the Hawaiian Islands rest, which means they seethe with activity. The giant Mauna Loa, built up from innumerable lava flows, towers 4,159 m (13,667 ft) above sea level. It first erupted in 1801 and its most recent activity was in 1984, when its 22-day eruption sent down lava flows over 26 km (16 miles). Kilauea, slightly smaller at 1,247 m (4,090 ft), has been studied more closely than any other volacano because of its spectacular history. In the 19th and early 20th centuries, it had an active lava lake, which disappeared in the explosion of 1924, when the size of the crater more than doubled. The most violent of modern eruptions was in November 1959 when a crack opened in the wall of the Kilauea Iki (Little Kilauea) crater (*see inset*) and the lava flew more than 300 m (1,000 ft) into the air. There is now a walking trail across the lava crust on the bottom of the crater. The lava lake floor is 110 m (360 ft) thick and steam billowing from every crack is a reminder that molten rock flows below.

Recently, the lava has flowed down into the village of Kalapana, destroying 150 homes, causing $25 million worth of damage and blocking the state highway. Where the lava reaches the sea, it creates a huge cloud of steam and the volcanic gases – mainly hydrogen, sulphur and silica – create a choking haze known as 'vog'. The road blockage has become a tourist attraction in itself and visitors can hike out across the rough blocks of lava until they stand on rock hot enough to burn the soles of their shoes. At night, the whole sky is suffused with a red glow. Since 1969, eruptions along the eastern rift of Kilauea have created a new lava shield called Mauna Ulu, 'Growing Mountain'. In its first five years, Mauna Ulu buried 19 km (12 miles) of road and 4,050 ha (10,000 acres) of land and built up a 122 m (400 ft) shield.

Hundreds of people flock to watch Hawaii's eruptions, for the main discharges are slow-moving lava flows and they do not produce the heavy clouds of ash that can prove catastrophic in other volcanic zones. 'Eruption bulletins' are issued daily. Scientists studying Kilauea are learning more about the way in which continents and islands have been created and destroyed, as well as improving methods of predicting future eruptions.

The Crater Rim Drive makes a 17.5 km (11 mile) circuit around the Kilauea caldera. The area is full of cinder cones, lava fields and steam vents as well as patches of lush vegetation. Devastation Trail leads through a dead forest, its trees roasted by the cinder fallout from the eruption. At Thurston lava tube, only a small section is open to the public as cave-ins further along have made it too dangerous, but walking through the tunnel of lava, with its arched ceiling burrowing into the fern-clad hillside, is an eerie experience. Lava tubes are formed when a crust forms over a hot lava flow, cooling and thickening while the lava within continues on its downhill course. The Thurston tube is by no means the largest found in Hawaii; they can be as high as 15 m (50 ft) and run for several kilometres. Also along the drive is a fern forest (though the area is drying up so the ferns are slowly disappearing), the Kau Desert, where the fine ash and lava resembles sand, and one of the two permanent volcano observatories in the USA. The Steam Vent walk gives a view over the rim of Kilauea, where steam spurts from every fissure, and winds past cracks where 19th century settlers used to steam chopped fern stumps until they were soft enough for pig food, to a great sulphur bank. The Chain of Craters Road runs 45 km (28 miles) past several enormous pit craters formed in prehistoric times as well as more recent lava flows. The landscape is like a frozen ocean of ripples, currents and wind-whipped water.

BORA BORA

James A. Michener thought Bora Bora 'the most beautiful island in the world' and used it as a model for his idyllic Pacific island, Bali Hai, though in fact when the film *South Pacific* was made, the mountain of Mou'aroa on Moorea, another of the islands of French Polynesia, was used as the actual location.

A barrier reef, dotted with sandy islets called *motus*, encircles Bora Bora's green shores, sheltering the colourful lagoon from the force of the Pacific breakers. The volcano responsible for the island's existence, which began to pile the lava of successive eruptions on the sea bed some 7 million years ago, still stands at its heart, its picturesque twin peaks the jagged remnants of the crater. The basalt peaks of long-extinct Mount Pahia stand nearly 660 m (2,165 ft), with Otemanu's unclimbable volcanic plug rising 65 m (214 ft) above it.

Bora Bora ('the first born') preserves its serenity in spite of the press of holidaymakers. The valleys are bright with hibiscus blooms, palm trees wave over sugary-white beaches, and snorkellers drift lazily through the many-hued gardens of coral, alive with tropical fish. Larger fish, an enormous variety of them – snapper, grouper, *mahi mahi*, yellowfin tuna, blue marlin – can be caught just outside the reef.

Ancient temples, called *maraes*, serve as reminders of the past. On the walls of Fare-Opu are carvings of turtles, considered sacred animals by the Polynesians and reserved as offerings for the gods or food for chiefs and priests on ceremonial occasions. Near the main temple, Marotetini, are the 19th century tombs of the Bora Bora royal family. Many human bones have been dug up in the area over the years and stories abound of the dire fate of anyone who removes them. One such vandal is reputed to have died in unexplained circumstances, his body charred as though he had burned to death.

Reminders of more recent history are the remains of coastal defences and gun emplacements from World War II. Following the attack on Pearl Harbor in 1942, the US government reviewed its strategy and decided that Bora Bora would serve as a useful refuelling base on the route from west coast America to Australia and New Zealand. In an operation codenamed 'Bobcat' several

thousand US naval and army personnel descended on the tiny island, setting up guns on the hillsides. Most of the troops were stationed in the area of Faanui Bay, a well-protected site where the base would be undetectable from the sea. The coming of the troops changed the traditional life of the islanders for ever, and when the base was closed in 1946 the effects on the economy of Bora Bora were devastating. Many half-caste babies, born during the brief occupation of the island, died from malnutrition when they were no longer able to obtain proprietary baby milk they were accustomed to. Since then, catering for tourists has become the principal business of Bora Bora's 4,000 inhabitants.

The original inhabitants of Bora Bora arrived around 2,000 years ago. Their ancestors had begun moving into the Pacific 1,000 years before that, making their famous voyages from south-east Asia. No one knows why these peoples left their homelands in such numbers, but the migration may have been caused by the expansion of the Chinese. The route they took is also in dispute. One theory is that they went first to Melanesia and from there gradually spread out to Polynesia; another is that they may have moved through the northern islands of Micronesia. Thor Heyerdahl, who proved the

possibility of crossing from Peru to eastern Polynesia by raft in his amazing Kon-Tiki expedition, believes that the migrants went first to America. Whatever route they chose, the Polynesian voyagers were highly skilled sailors navigating their huge canoes by the sun and the stars, reading the movement of the waters and the clouds.

European explorers first came in the 18th century, though it took many years to discover and map the 130 islands of Polynesia. The English explorer James Cook made three expeditions between 1768 and 1779, charting the islands of Bora Bora, Huahine, and Tahaa. In 1769 he named them the Society Islands, because they were so close to one another. In 1880, the Society Islands were annexed by France, becoming part of French Polynesia.

Charles Darwin, author of *The Origin of Species*, studied Bora Bora's reef as part of the development of his theory of atolls. It had been thought that these circular reefs formed on the rim of underwater volcanoes. Darwin decided that an atoll began as a barrier reef round an island but was left behind as the island gradually sank into the sea. The island of Bora Bora is sinking slowly and, in the distant future, only an atoll will remain.

EUROPE

The Central Alps, near Klosters, Switzerland

THE DOLOMITES

The jagged needles and thrusting pinnacles of the Dolomites, a mountain group in the Italian Alps near the Austrian border, take their name from their rock. They are composed of hard, crystalline dolomite, limestone with a small proportion of magnesium carbonate, first identified in 1789 by the French geologist Dolomieu. The rock is predominantly pinky-grey, though its sparkling surface sometimes shines almost white. At a touch, a salty white powder comes away on the fingers, a reminder that the Dolomites originated as a coral reef below the sea. The special beauty of these mountains comes from the contrast between the fantastic shapes of the dolomite rocks cut by erosion and the gentle marl slopes on which they rest.

The wild landscape of the mountain heights offers a challenge of dizzy pinnacles, vertical chimneys and precipices to rock climbers. The highest peak, Marmolada, is 3,341 m (10,961 ft) and 17 other peaks rise to more than 3,000 m (9,850 ft). At the same time, the lower slopes are hospitable, clothed in pine forests and meadows bright with wild flowers in spring and early summer. Vineyards are laid out to catch the sun on the hillsides and fruit trees flourish in the valleys. By May the snow is gone and the crisp, dry air makes the mountains a pleasant summer retreat. Mountain centres like Belluno, Trento, Bolzano and Merano, open to the sun and sheltered from the cold, remain warm even through autumn.

Cortina d'Ampezzo, with its ideal position in a sunny meadow at the junction of two valleys, has been a major winter sports centre for decades and claims to have staged the world's first skiing contest. A ring of five mountains surround the town: Cristallo with its cathedral-like shape, Sorapis with tongue-like ridges, the five battlemented towers of Cinque Torri, Civetta looking like a stiff sentinal and Pelmo, the 'throne of God'. Nearby, across the Tre Croci Pass, is the brilliantly-coloured Lake Misurina, one of the loveliest of the mountain lakes.

One of Italy's most spectacular motoring experiences, the Great Dolomites Road, runs between Cortina and Bolzano. This climbs first to the top of Boite valley for a view over the resort, then past the steep slopes of the Tofane with its first-class ski runs and through

the tunnel at Passa di Falzarego. It switchbacks to Canazei, below the Marmolada group, and through the Fassa Valley. Before the narrow gorge of the Val d'Ega, the road is sandwiched between the peaks of the Latemar group and the towering face of the Rosengarten.

According to legend the fantastic crests and walls of the Rosengarten were the rose garden of Laurin, King of the Dwarfs, who became involved in a battle over the theft of a woman from the valleys and was eventually overpowered and imprisoned. He put a curse on the roses, turning them into rocks and vowing that if he could not look on them no one else would ever see them, by night or by day. However, he forgot to mention dawn or dusk and at these times the roses still bloom, casting their reds and pinks on the rock of the mountain.

The town of Bolzano looks more Austrian than Italian, with its Tyrolean-style houses and arcaded streets. Most people in the area – known either as Alto Adige or Süd Tirol – speak two languages. From the 14th century the region was ruled by the Hapsburgs and Napoleon placed it formally in the hands of Austria. However, Italy gained Trentino at the end of World War I and over the next few years its frontier expanded as far as the Brenner Pass. The towns were given Italian names and Italian was taught in all schools. Some bitterness still lingers from these times, with extreme separatist groups causing trouble from time to time and many of the people of this region feeling less than wholeheartedly Italian.

Not all the inhabitants of the Dolomites speak either German or Italian; for some the language is Ladin or Romansch. These, the Ladini, some 16,000 of whom live in valleys such as Val Gardena and the Val Badia, are the descendants of Roman soldiers sent by the Emperor Tiberius to conquer the Celtic peoples of the Swiss mountain valleys and the Tirol. After their victory the soldiers sent for their families and settled down to await further orders, which never came. The Ladini lived in isolation until recent times and their original Latin evolved separately from Italian.

To the south of the land of the Ladini, on the far side of the Marmolada group, lies one of the most peaceful, untouched areas of the Dolomites, within the National Park Paneveeggio. The magnificent rolling forests, once the source of timber for Venetian ships, are a refuge for wildlife and a tranquil wilderness.

MOUNT VESUVIUS

Goethe described Vesuvius as the 'peak of hell rising out of paradise'. It stands above the tranquil Bay of Naples, its lower slopes clothed in orchards and vineyards and with its upper reaches desolate and threatening. The eruptions of this still active volcano have already killed thousands of people, yet a population of more than 2 million continually live within its reach. In the fertile volcanic soil of the foothills grow quantities of egg-shaped Marzano tomatoes and the vineyards producing 'Lacrima Christi' wine are found here.

Vesuvius stands at about 1,280 m (4,200 ft), its height varying slightly from year to year, and its summit is a huge caldera more than 3 km (2 miles) across. On the northern side of the volcano is the precipice called Monte Somma, a remnant of the ancient rim, separated from the current crater by a hollow, the Atrio del Cavallo. Within the crater wisps of smoke curl lazily and the guides for the tourists light their cigarettes in hot pockets in the soil.

Vesuvius has a history of eruptions stretching back 12,000 years, but its most famous explosion was in AD 79 when it destroyed the towns of Pompeii and Herculaneum, leaving behind a priceless archaeological legacy. At the time, inhabitants of the flourishing commercial centres on the bay believed that the volcano was extinct and the eruption of 24 August caught them tragically unprepared. The first intimation of disaster was a violent earthquake, then an ear-splitting blast as the volcano burst open and a tremendous black cloud rose skyward. Hot ash and pumice rained down on Pompeii and poisonous gas was released into the air. Only one in four of the population managed to escape; the rest were buried alive by hot ash, suffocated by sulphurous fumes or crushed by collapsing buildings. For two days ash and cinders rained down, burying the city beneath what looked like a blanket of grey snow. Though Herculaneum, a small coastal town to the west of Pompeii, escaped the dust and fumes, heavy rains brought down an avalanche of volcanic mud, burying the town to a depth of 18 m (60 ft).

The survivors, terrified by the destruction they had witnessed, made no attempt to rebuild their homes and the site was abandoned. The ruins of Pompeii were rediscovered by chance in the

18th century but it was only in 1861 that systematic excavations were begun and the city was resurrected, street by street, to give a unique glimpse of its life and death. Decomposing bodies had left impressions within the enveloping ash. and plaster casts taken from the cavities give a vivid picture of the last moments of some of the inhabitants, including a whole family clinging together and a pregnant woman lying on her stomach, trying to protect her unborn child. In the houses were carbonized loaves, eggs in eggcups, pots and pans ready on the hearth. Statues, wall paintings, gardens and fountains show the prosperity of the city.

Since then, Vesuvius has erupted 40 times, though vulcanologists believe that it went through a dormant period for 600 years after the lava flow of 1037. The most serious explosion was in 1631, when 3,000 people died. Though the earth had been rumbling with small quakes all summer, the warnings were ignored and on 17 December two rifts appeared in the southwestern side of the mountain and red-hot lava poured out. It rolled on, covering six villages, while nine others were engulfed in mud.

One of the earliest attempts to study the structure of Vesuvius was made by the British diplomat Sir William Hamilton. He was in Naples during the 1767 eruption, and from his villa he was able to watch a subsidiary cone building within the crater. He even climbed the mountain for a closer look but was driven back by heat and fumes and had to content himself with keeping a daily record of activity and sending samples of volcanic rock for analysis in London. Over the next 30 years, Hamilton made many journeys to view the crater, corresponding with the President of the Royal Society over his findings and finally publishing the correspondence in book form as a valuable contribution to the study of volcanoes.

Vesuvius demonstrated its destructive power again in 1906, when the crater widened by 300 m (1,000 ft). One of the towns destroyed by the lava from this explosion was Boscotrecase, where a geologist reported 'houses have been overturned, displaced or buried. . . . In some engulfed houses the flow was fluid enough to penetrate all the doors, windows and gratings facing the volcano and fill the rooms. There was one house where it had actually begun to mount the stairs.' The most recent substantial eruption was in 1944, but there were no fatalities. Scientists say that it is only a matter of time before the volcano wakes again.

THE AUVERGNE

The long line of extinct volcanoes that forms the Auvergne lies at the heart of France's Massif Central (mountains far older than the Alps or the Pyrenees) and is its most remarkable feature. The Parc Régional Naturel des Volcans d'Auvergne, created in 1977 to protect this distinctive region, stretches from the Monts Dômes in the north, through the high barrier of the Monts Dore to the hills of Cantal. There are hundreds of 'puys', or peaks; some sharp, some weathered by time into softly rounded hills, their gentle cones vivid green against a great expanse of sky. Some of the craters hold lakes, some have densely forested hillsides, while others have been blasted almost out of existence by long-ago eruptions.

The Monts Dore are the youngest of the volcanic chains, thrown up about 1 million years ago. Volcanic activity here continued until 4,000 years ago and the puys are still sharp little cones, scores of them rearing a few hundred metres above the plateau. The highest is Puy de Dôme (*see inset*), a flat-topped peak 1,465 m (4,806 ft) high,

and from the summit reached by a toll road or on foot on a pathway dating from Roman times, there is a view over 50 or more puys, stretching out into the distance, the fertile volcanic soil between them deeply wooded. The Puy de Dôme is composed of porous trachyte, but it was recognized as an extinct volcano only in the mid-18th century, as its mass hardened immediately after emerging from the ground, leaving no crater. An observatory on the summit dwarfs the remnants of a Temple of Mercury, the messenger of the gods, excavated in 1873.

The volcanoes of the Monts Dore and the Cantal are much older and the faulting and rifting here was more violent. The summit of central France is the Puy de Sancy, standing 1,885 m (6,184 ft) high in the Monts Dore and commanding a panoramic view. Below is the town of Mont-Dore itself, popular as a spa in Roman times and set in a beautiful amphitheatre of mountains. To the south, the Cantal mountains are the last remains of a single huge primeval volcano. The highest remnant is the Plomb du Cantal, 1,855 m (6,086 ft), the tallest edge of the ruined crater, though the Puy Mary at 1,787 m (5,863 ft) almost matches it.

Outside the area of the park is a further volcanic region, the

Velay, centred on Le Puy, the least-visited part of the Massif Central. Narrow needles of volcanic rock stand sentinel at Le Puy. On the Rocher Corneille is a mammoth 19th century statue of the Virgin Mary, called Notre-Dame-de-France and weighing 110 tonnes. On Rocher St Michel perches the Romanesque 11th-century St Michael's chapel. Both look down on the old town and the cathedral, where medieval pilgrims made the steep climb on worship the Black Virgin. Many still come, though the image of the Virgin on the high altar is only a copy; the original was publicly burned during the Revolution.

The Auvergne is one of the most sparsely populated regions in France. Traditional industries have declined and young people frequently move away, leaving an aging population. The capital is the grey volcanic stone city of Clermont-Ferrand, which became the centre of the rubber tyre industry in the later 19th century. The Romans settled here, calling it Augustonemetum and it was given its present name, from the 'bright mountain' of Puy de Dôme, only in 1731.

The region takes its name from the Arverni, a Gallic tribe whose stronghold was at Gergovia, near Clermont-Ferrand. Their chieftain, Vercingetorix, succeeded in uniting the Gallic tribes for the first time in his opposition to Julius Caesar and the advance of the Roman legions in 53 BC. Though he won a pitched battle on the steep basalt Plateau de Gergovie, 10 km (6 miles) outside Clermont-Ferrand, he unwisely continued to fight the Romans across Burgundy, where he was defeated and captured. Under the Romans, the Auvergne was part of Aquitania Prima. Later, powerful feudal lords controlled the region. For several centuries local wars were common and when the noble lords were not fighting, their soldiers had plenty of time to pillage the countryside. Peasants and traders frequently found their crops and goods seized by the soldiers or confiscated by the nobles. Under Louis XIV, a travelling court was set up to discipline the lords and restore some semblance of order. Through the 17th and 18th centuries, a succession of governors was sent to build up the economy of the Auvergne, which had stagnated owing to the constant unrest of the population. To be governor of this region was recognized as a particularly tough assignment and successful governors were assured of advancement, as it was understood that a man who could govern the fiercely independent Auvergne was able to govern anywhere.

DARTMOOR

The granite mass of Dartmoor is the largest and highest of five such masses at the heart of southern England, with an average elevation of 366 m (1,200 ft). It is the remnant of a mountain system 3 million years old, its granite mainly made up of porphyritic feldspar, but also containing quartz, tourmaline and black and white mica. Most of the moorland granite has weathered into gently rolling hills and wide green valleys. However, the differing constituents of the granite, combined with its situation, mean that some areas have been more resistant to weathering then others. To the east, the ground does not rise more than 366 m (1,200 ft) above sea level. In the south, some hills rise a further 122 m (400 ft) but the highest points of the moor are in the north, where High Willhays stands 621 m (2,039 ft) and Yes Tor 618 m (2,028 ft).

In many places regal lumps of unyielding granite have remained intact as the ground rotted away around them, standing as solid outcrops (*see below*) or as 'tors' crowning the hillsides. In Gaelic, 'torr' means simply a mound or hill and the famous moorland tors – 200 of them – vary widely in character. Vixen Tor can look like a fox, or a sphinx or even a witch, according the angle of light. On Coombestone Tor the rock-piles look man-made, as though labourers of ancient times had stacked them to make walls. Longaford Tor rises on a ridge like a castle, Hay Tor is known for its humps, Staple Tor has rocks rising like steeples and Bellever Tor (*see inset*) has a scattering of sturdy blocks along the hillside. The east moor has a noble semi-circle of tors within easy walking distance of one another: Hound Tor, Honeybag Tor, Chinkwell Tor, Rippon Tor, Saddle Tor and Hay Tor. Often the tops of rocks are hollowed out by millions of years of freezes and thaws; for instance, Yes Tor holds a deep basin, its rounded sides the result of weathering.

A wealth of prehistoric monuments is scattered across the moor. They owe their survival partly to the lack of devlopment in the area, partly to the fact that the most easily available building material was the highly durable granite. The earliest monuments are megalithic tombs, dating from around 2000 BC. These were communal burial

chambers, long cairns or mounds marked by huge upright slabs and topped by capstones. At South Brent the cairn is 40 m (130 ft) long. Bronze Age burials were individual rather than communal and marked by round stone cairns, sometimes solitary on a rise, sometimes grouped together like those on Butterdon Hill, near Ivybridge.

From the early Bronze Age come the twelve stone circles, probably erected for ceremonial use, and the rows of stones, or 'alignments', which may extend for as much as 1.6 km (1 mile). The rows usually lead to a cairn, so scholars believe they must have marked a funerary way to the tomb. The villages, collections of little round huts, and the pounds, surrounded by huge walls, date from later in the Bronze Age. The most famous of the pounds is Grimspound, where walls 1.8 m (6 ft) high and 2.7 m (9 ft) thick, built to keep the cattle safe from predators, enclose a settlement of 24 huts.

There seems to have been a lull in the occupation of Dartmoor from Roman times onwards. The existence of Dartmoor was not recorded in the Domesday Book. In 1240 its boundaries were marked out when it was officially a 'royal forest', which meant that it was reserved as one of the king's hunting grounds. The moor remained undisturbed until the presence of tin was discovered in the 12th century. Miners moved in, farmers came too and new villages grew up. The remnants of one of these medieval villages has been excavated between Hound Tor and Great Tor. It seems to have been deserted in the 14th century when the Black Death ravaged the moorland settlements. In medieval times, when the new settlements meant that people were travelling over the difficult moorland terrain, granite crosses were set up to mark the tracks. A number, like Marchant's Cross near Meavy, still stand. The clapper bridges, made from huge stones, like the one crossing the River Dart at Postbridge, also made travelling easier.

In modern times, large amounts of granite were quarried on Dartmoor. Moorland quarries supplied several hundred types of granite. It was used for many of the handsome churches in the area, for rebuilding London Bridge in 1825, for the forbidding Dartmoor Prison and for Nelson's Column in London's Trafalgar Square. The industry declined in the late 19th century but even so Dartmoor granite has an unassailable place in history.

THE GIANT'S CAUSEWAY

The Giant's Causeway looks so much like a man-made structure that many early visitors, making the difficult journey by boat or on horseback after hearing of its great wonders, were disappointed, feeling that they had been deceived. However, man had no hand in forming Northern Ireland's most famous sight, the extraordinary Causeway of basalt columns stretching from the cliff face out into the sea. The columns had their beginnings 60 million years ago with the volcanic eruption that formed the Antrim plateau. The lava in the centre of the flow cooled more slowly than lava above and below, and contraction caused hexagonal cracks which formed into a remarkably regular set of columns.

The basalt promontory is divided into three sections: the Little, Middle and the Grand Causeway, 12 m (40 ft) wide as it leaves the cliff, gradually narrowing as it runs for 91 m (300 ft) before disappearing under the waves. The formations look so much like enormous stepping stones that in Irish mythology they are the beginning of a pathway built by Finn MacCool, the great warrior and commander of the king's army, planned to link-up with the coast of Scotland 48 km (30 miles) away, so that he could cross without getting his feet wet.

Before the Causeway became a tourist attraction, local peasants used to use the exposed joints, where the columns have split, as salt pans, filling them with sea water then scraping out the salt once the water had evaporated in the sun. Its fame spread in the 18th century, after reports and illustrations were published by the Royal Society and the Dublin Society. At the time, there was fierce controversy over the origins of the Causeway. One scientific school, known as the Neptunists, believed that it was sedimentary rock, its formations caused by chemical precipitation within water, and that the Causeway had had its origins in the flood of the Old Testament. The Vulcanists, however, insisted that its origin was the result of volcanic action. It was only in the 19th century that the latters' theory was widely accepted.

In 1740 the well-known artist Susanne Drury painted two pictures of the causeway, one from the east side and the other from the west, and they sold widely throughout Europe, firing interests in this lonely section of the Irish coast. However, the journey discouraged all but the most adventurous. When Boswell tried to persuade Dr Johnson to visit Ireland, he asked: 'Is not the Giant's Causeway worth seeing?' 'Worth seeing? Yes, but not worth going to see', answered the great man. It was the opening of the coast road from Larne to Portrush in 1837 that brought the tourists flooding in. Later, in 1883, the first hydroelectric tramway in the world was opened between Portrush and the Causeway.

With no National Trust to protect it in the 18th century, the Causeway was overrun with locals-turned-guides and all manner of hawkers and stalls. The English write William Makepeace Thackeray was appalled by the scene, as he was attacked from all sides by pushing, shouting guides, and narrowly missed being pulled down a precipice. He found himself hauled into a boat and thoroughly soaked as he was rowed out into a rough sea: 'Before I had leisure to ask myself why the deuce, I was in the boat with four rowers hurrooing and bounding madly from one huge liquid mountain to another – four rowers whom I was bound to pay'. It is hardly surprising that, after such an experience, his view of the Causeway was somewhat jaundiced: 'Mon Dieu! and have I travelled a hundred miles to see that?'

Most modern visitors marvel at the expanse of 37,000 columns, filling 2 ha (5 acres). The vast majority are hexagons, though a few are 4, 5 or 7-sided and two, the Key Stone and the Wishing Chair, have 8 sides. Other formations have descriptive names like the Chimney Pots, the Punchbowl, the Giant's Pot Lid, and My Lady's Fan. An 8 km (5 mile) circular walk takes in the Causeway itself and the surrounding bays, passing the Giant's Amphitheatre with its half-circle of towering pillars and the Giant's Organ, its 60 regular columns 12 m (39 ft) tall. The cliffs all along the coast in this region are a geologist's delight, as it is possible to identify many different strata, the older rock having been protected for millions of years by a covering layer of lava.

The adjoining bay is called Port na Spaniagh, where the Spanish Armada ship *Girona* was wrecked in 1588, with the death of all but 5 out of 1,300 men. In the 1960s a party of Belgian divers located the ship's treasure, which included hundreds of gold and silver coins, gold jewellery set with precious stones and valuable silver tableware. The best of the treasure is now housed in the Ulster Museum, Belfast.

STAFFA

Fisherman of the Inner Herbrides had their own Gaelic name for the cave formed by columnar basalt on the island of Staffa ('the isle of staves'); they called it simply 'musical cave'. They had all heard the haunting, Aeolian harp effects of air currents among the basalt pillars. It was this sound that inspired Mendelssohn to compose the overture 'Fingal's Cave'. 'What a wonder is Fingal's Cave', he wrote in his diary after his visit in 1829. 'This vast cathedral of the sea with its dark lapping waves within, and the brightness of the gleaming waves outside. . .'.

The cave was unknown to the outside world until it was visited by Joseph Banks, later President of the Royal Society, in 1772. Banks was on an expedition bound for Iceland when his party spent a night at Mull and he heard of the local curiosity. He was thrilled by what he found as his boat approached the island. 'Compared to this what are the cathedrals and palaces built by men! Mere models or playthings, imitations as diminutive as his works will always be when compared with those of nature . . . in a short time we arrived at the mouth of a cave, the most magnificent, I suppose, that has ever been described by travellers.'

When his find was written up in the *Scots Magazine*, Banks claimed that his local guide told him that the place was known as the Cave of Finn, though it seems likely that he misheard the Gaelic name, *Uaimh Binn*, the 'musical cave'. His assumption that it was linked with the legendary hero Finn MacCool, or Fingal, is not all that surprising, for Fingal was a well-known character in England at the time. A young poet, James Macpherson, had published what he claimed as the translation of a long-lost Gaelic work, *Fingal: an Ancient Epic Poem*. The poem, supposedly the work of Ossian, Fingal's son, caught the public imagination. Banks's name for the cave, and its obvious similarity to the already well-known Giant's Causeway on the coast of Northern Ireland, gave rise to the story of a pathway built by Fingal between Antrim and Staffa, so that he could reach an old enemy who lived in the cave.

News of the splended cave tempted many famous visitors.

Wordsworth came and so did Sir Walter Scott. Keats was so impressed that he wrote 'for solemnity and grandeur it far surpasses the finest cathedral'. The painter Turner insisted on jumping from a boat unable to land in rough weather and disappeared inside the cave for three hours while a boatload of seasick passengers was tossed back and forth on the angry waves. The result was the painting *Staffa: Fingal's Cave*, which fetched a high price in New York in 1845. In 1847 Queen Victoria herself visited Staffa, together with Prince Albert and her two eldest children, while on a tour of the Hebrides. The Queen's barge, its royal standard flying, was solemnly rowed into the cave by its crew of oarsmen, while a cluster of larger boats gathered round the tiny island.

Staffa is about 1.6 km (1 mile) long and its highest point is 41 m (135 ft) above the water. The densely stacked columns that form the island date back to volcanic disturbances that found a weakness in the earth's crust aeons ago and ejected large amounts of molten basalt along a line from the Antrim coast to Skye. The basalt can be seen through Rathlin, Islay and Mull, as well as Staffa. This volcanic activity has been dated to the Eocene period, some 70 million years ago, by plant remains found in some localities.

A tongue of hexagonal columns leads to the mouth of the cave, and halfway along is the formation known as Fingal's Chair, said to grant three wishes to anyone who sits there. A magnificent archway forms the entrance to the grotto, which penetrates 60 m (200 ft) into the island. It is about 18 m (60 ft) high and tapers from 13 m (42 ft) at the opening to 6 m (20 ft) at the far end. The musical sounds are heard at high tide, when the rising water compresses air in the cave.

When Banks visited Staffa he was entertained by its single inhabitant, who provided fish and milk and 'sang all night in the Erse language, which we did not understand'. By the time the French geologist St Fond arrived in 1784, there were two families on the island, but by the mid-19th century it was uninhabited. In the late 1960s there were plans to build a tourist complex on the island but strenuous opposition came from the National Trust, the Countryside Commission and the Nature Conservancy, so planning permission was denied and the disappointed owner sold the island for £20,000.

VATNAJÖKULL

Geologically, Iceland is a young country. It has been thrown up from the sea-bed over the past 50 million years by the intense activity of the Mid-Atlantic Ridge. The Ridge is a volcanic mountain range, most of it below the sea, which has filled a long fissure in the earth's crust caused by the tearing apart of the North American and Eurasian plates. Iceland is still growing and changing with the restless movement below. The island has around 200 volcanoes and there is, on average, an eruption every five years. The fiery mountains have pitted, scarred and twisted the barren landscape with craters, jagged crags of lava and immense sheets of grey basalt. Iceland is a country of violent contrasts. The climate, with extremes of temperatures, leads to the ready accumulation of snow and ice, and one eighth of the island is under a permanent sheet of ice. It is the combination of fire and ice that provides the most spectacular demonstrations of natural power.

The greatest of the ice-caps is Vatnajökull, which covers 8,420 sq km (3,250 sq miles) with its peaks, craters, glaciers and lakes. The ice averages 420 m (1,378 ft) thick, but in places it goes down to more than 1,000 m (3,280 ft). To the east, the ice covers basalt formations from volcanic eruptions over 1 million years ago; to the west it lies across recent lava flows, some of which have taken place beneath the ice. The highest reaches of Vatnajökull cover mountain peaks and calderas. The most amazing of these calderas is Grimsvötn, cradling a hot lake 488 m (1,600 ft) deep from which it takes its name, 'Water of Odin'. The lake has a covering of ice 200 m (656 ft) thick but the lower layers are gradually melted by the heat so that the volume of the lake swells. Eventually the water rises so high that it lifts the ice and breaks out in a violent torrent known as a *jökulhlaup*, carrying such a force of water, mud and stones that it sweeps away everything in its path. In 1934 the burst was so violent that the volume of water being discharged reached an amazing 50,000 cu m (1.8 million cu ft) per second and the floods lasted for a week. Icebergs 20 m (66 ft) high were swept along with the other debris; the places where they settled into the ground and eventually melted can still be seen as 'kettle holes'. These glacier bursts used to happen every ten years, but now that the climate has warmed and the glaciers are shrinking it takes only five years for sufficient pressure to build up, so that the water breaks through the barrier of ice.

In the south of Vatnajökull is the caldera of another volcano, Öraefajökull and one of its ragged peaks is the highest in Iceland at 2,120 m (6,955 ft). There is still a live core of magma beneath the volcano, which may one day erupt again. It was last active in 1727 but it was the massive explosion of 1362 that laid waste the region, burying it beneath a thick layer of mud, pumice and ash, demolishing every building and killing all vegetation. The eruption has become part of Icelandic folklore and the story goes that a farmer called Hallur was the only survivor. He was milking cows when he heard two thunderous crashes coming from the mountain and, leaving the cows, he fled for shelter in a cave. Everyone else in the locality perished as the third and greatest crash came. In the coastal area below the glacier there are few farms and no ports: it is called Öraefasveit, the 'uninhabited wasteland'. Before the construction of the road running right round the island, this area was isolated from the rest of the country. Road construction was a long and difficult business here, because the many rivers running down from the glacier frequently flood and change course so that half-completed sections of the road were often washed away.

The best access to the glacier is from Skaftafell National Park, established in 1968. Ice from the great ice-cap above feeds the Skaftafellsjökull, and many interesting glacial features can be seen here: old meltwater channels, marks scoured into the rock cliffs caused by ice scraping past and, at the end of the glacier, large crevasses with ridges of ice between them. The snout of the glacier is black because the glacier is retreating, so that there is a large proportion of black sand in the diminishing ice at this point. It is also possible to scale the highest peak of Öraefajökull, starting from the park. Another reminder of past volcanoes is the waterfall of Svartifoss, which falls through a semi-circle of organ-pipe basalt formations. The geometric lines of Svartifoss inspired the design for Reykjavík's National Theatre.

STROKKUR

It was Iceland's great Geysir, the 'Great Gusher', that gave the term geyser to the world. In its heyday, it was the largest of a cluster of geysers and sent up great jets of water more than 61 m (200 ft) high and 3 m (10 ft) in diameter. It was recognized as a marvel 800 years ago, when those who witnessed its power thought that the boiling water came straight from hell. In the 19th century it was a famous tourist sight and performed regularly, but by the early years of this century it had stopped gushing. Though it has sprung into activity occasionally since then, Geysir today is a still pool of blue water, cradled in a cone of silicates.

Now the big draw is provided by a neighbouring geyser, Strokkur, 'the Churn' (*below and inset*), which erupts several times every hour. Its hot water comes up a 2 m (6 ft) pipe into a steaming pool about 10 m (32 ft) in diameter. As the pool fills, all is quiet, then the water starts heaving until the pressure from below forces up a smooth bubble of water which suddenly breaks and sends up a narrow column up to 40 m (131 ft) high. The steam clouds take seconds to disperse and by then the waters have subsided again.

Geysers, deep cylindrical holes full of water, get their energy from the heat of molten volcanic rocks below the earth's surface. Some constriction or bend within the long tube of the geyser prevents the water from circulating freely. Though water boils at 100′C (212°F) under normal atmospheric pressure, the boiling point rises under extra pressure, so that the water trapped down in the tube reaches temperatures far higher than the normal boiling point and a little of this is converted into steam. The water expands as it vaporizes so that the top of the geyser overflows. This in turn lowers the pressure, enabling more of the water to turn to steam, which bursts out of the vent carrying a jet of boiling water high into the air.

At one time, the Gusher was persuaded to perform by throwing quantities of soap into the tube. The soap turns the surface of the water into lighter bubbles, which lessens pressure artificially and stimulates the geyser into action – foaming at the mouth as the water bubbles more and more violently, then ejecting its stream of

water. Recently artificial methods of persuasion have been discouraged and visitors have to be content with the ever-reliable Strokkur.

Both Geysir and Strokkur have built up extensive deposits of silica from successive eruptions. The waters of geysers, like those of mineral springs, contain various salts, most often carbonates, chlorides and sulphates. As the water evaporates and cools it deposits some of the minerals held in solution and these build up into mounds, cones or terraces, adding to the attractive appearance of thermal areas.

Iceland has 800 geothermal areas and hundreds of springs with an average water temperature of 75:C (167°F). Some of this underground energy has been tapped for practical purposes: the capital, Reykjavik, is a 'smokeless city', with all its industrial and domestic heating provided by natural hot water. At the turn of the century the city's inhabitants often took their week's laundry out to the hot springs a few kilometres away and in some areas it was possible to make bread by burying the prepared dough in a pit hollowed out of the ground. Then, in the 1920s, the first pipes were laid to begin exploiting geothermal power. Now almost all Reykjavik homes use the pure hot water that flows from the ground. The city, after decades free from the pollution caused by other forms of power, looks sparklingly clean. East of the city, at Hveragerdhi, the 'garden of hot springs', the springs have been heating glasshouses (greenhouses) growing all forms of salad vegetables, as well as bananas and grapes, roses and orchids, since the 1930s.

Lake Mývatn, the fifth largest lake in Iceland and the most famous, was damned by a lava flow and is fed by hot springs. The surrounding mountains steam and the shores are dotted with small lava cones, the result of eruptions that destroyed almost all the buildings around the lake in the 1720s. The warm waters make it a haven for birds; in summer more than 150,000 ducks make their home on the lake and more species are found here than anywhere else in the world. The hot springs supply minerals which help single-celled algae called diatoms to flourish and the skeltons of these diatoms form a thick sediment on the shallow bed of the lake. This sediment is pumped out of Mývatn and piped to a geothermally powered factory to be used in various industrial processes, including the manufacture of photographic film and gunpowder.

THE MIDNIGHT SUN

The phenomenon of the 'midnight sun' occurs in the polar regions where, for part of the year, the sun never disappears below the horizon. It is caused by the tilting of the earth's axis, which governs the length of day or night throughout the world. Though countries near the Equator have days and nights of roughly the same duration all the year round, those nearer to the poles have greater variations: the nearer they are to the North or South poles, the greater the variation.

As the earth revolves around the sun, in every 24-hour period it makes the sun appear to rise and set at regular intervals, causing periods of 'day' and 'night'. If the earth's axis were vertical, these periods would last a regular 12 hours. However, as the axis is tilted, it causes one pole and then the other to slant towards the sun. This means that the sun never sets at the North Pole for six months beginning in late March. It remains swinging in the sky, increasing in altitude until midsummer day, then decreasing in altitude until it slides around the horizon in September, seen for a while as a day-long sunset. Then the poles change places and from late September the sun does not set for six months at the South Pole.

Anywhere north of the 66th parallel, the sun does not set on midsummer day, and in many countries midsummer eve is a time of celebration, with all-night parties, barbecues and plenty of alcohol. This is a relic of an ancient pagan festival, though in Scandinavian countries, for example, it is now dedicated to John the Baptist (generally known as St Hans) to give it respectability. Among the most popular customs are bonfires set on hill-tops, beside lakes and along the seashore, with displays of fireworks let off as dusk turns to dawn. On a clear night the midnight sun is a magnificent spectacle; even on a cloudy night its red globe glows in the sky. In some countries people still join hands in a circle and sing as they walk round and round the bonfire. Maypoles, too, are symbols of mid-summer, their name coming not from the month of May, but from an Old Norse word meaning 'to decorate'. In the Åland islands, lying between Finland and Sweden, where the inhabitants are proud of their folk customs, the maypoles are still tall and extremely elaborate, entwined with garlands of flowers and topped by flags or windmills.

The length of time during which the midnight sun is experienced depends, of course, on latitude. At the Arctic Circle, it lasts for only a few days around 21 December. In Norway, where this picture was taken, the period varies: Tromsø enjoys the midnight sun from 21 May to 23 July; at the North Cape it shines between 12 May and 29 July; and in Spitzbergen the period lasts from 21 April to 22 August.

The summer effect of the midnight sun is balanced in the other half of the year by days of continuous darkness. North of the 70th parallel there is no sun at all from mid-November to mid-January. In much of Scandinavia the beginning of the long, dark nights is heralded by All Saints' Eve on 1 November. Norwegians call it the 'murky time'.

In medieval times, the Scandinavian countries were known as the 'midnight lands', a far less romantic name than the 'land of the midnight sun' advertised in tourist brochures. Early travellers went home with frightening tales of the endless darkness and intense cold of the northern winters. These winters have always had a profound psychological effect on those who have to live through months without light or sunshine. Scandinavian folk-lore is full of doom and gloom and in modern times a depression known as the 'dark sickness' in Scandinavia is a recognized complaint.

THE FJORDS OF NORWAY

During the last Ice Age, some 3 million years ago, a vast ice sheet covered the whole of Scandinavia. Within the ice, huge glaciers moved, carried on thin films of meltwater, seeking out any surface faults in the land, moving along rock fractures or existing river valleys which had already been widened by previous glaciation. The glaciers swept up all loose debris along their paths, increasing the scouring power of the ice by incorporating such debris in the main mass, then gouging out the floor of the valleys and penetrating deep into every crack in the bedrock, plucking out and transporting huge blocks of rock.

The steep-sided, flat-bottomed fjords of western Norway are the sites of ancient river systems, exploited by glaciers. When the ice eventually melted, the sea rushed in to fill the deep troughs left behind. The same fjord can vary greatly in depth; at its mouth it may be only 18 m (60 ft) deep but inland it may be ten times deeper. Ice moving down from the uplands often built up at the head of the valley, or along its course, wherever its bulk was greatly increased by glaciers joining from tributaries of the original river. As it was unable to escape, it burrowed deeper and deeper into the trough. At the head of the valley, where the land on the banks of the trough was lower, some of the ice was able to spill over and disperse, easing the pressure.

For most visitors, the fjords are the epitome of Norway. They are sometimes starkly dramatic, their cliffs rising vertically from the water, with no strip of land offering a foothold for human habitation. Waterfalls cascade down their sides and snow clad peaks rise beyond. Elsewhere, lush green fields border the water.

The fjords begin around Stavanger, the commercial centre for the surrounding area, which gained extra importance in recent years from the offshore oil-fields of the North Sea. East of the town is Lysefjord, a 37 km (23 mile) long gash in the mountains hemmed in by 1,000 m (3,280 ft) cliffs, described by Victor Hugo as 'the most dreadful of all the corridor rocks in the sea'. High above it stands the Prekestolen, the 'Pulpit Rock', reached by a two-hour moorland climb and providing a wide-ranging view out towards the western fjords.

Hardangerfjord, south of Bergen, is a wide fjord with many complex branches and peninsulas, and some of Norway's richest farmland lies along its lower reaches. Half a million fruit trees, mainly apple and cherry, grow in orchards alongside the water, blanketing the banks with pink and white blossom in late May. Hardanger is famous for its waterfalls, which have inspired artists for 150 years: Skykkjedalsfoss is the tallest in Norway at 300 m (984 ft), but Vøringfoss, 183 m (600 ft), is one of the most beautiful, crashing into a narrow cleft in the rocks, its cloud of spray catching the light in multi-coloured rainbows. At the lower falls of Steinsdalsfoss it is possible to walk behind the sheet of tumbling water. Above is the mountain plateau of Hardangervidda, where herds of wild reindeer graze and 120 species of birds breed.

No roads run the full length of Sognefjord, 30 km (50 miles) above Bergen. This is the country's longest and deepest fjord, biting into the land for 200 km (124 miles). It lies 1,220 m (4,002 ft) below the surrounding plateau and its main arm is 800 m (2,625 ft) deep. One of its many branches is Aurlandsfjord (*see below*), where the warmer, wetter climate nurtures orchards of apricots and peaches on delta land formed by the sea flowing in as the ice melted and

building up thick deposits of gravel and mud. The western branch of Aurlandsfjord is Naerøyfjord, so hemmed in by cliffs that for half the year the sun never reaches the water.

Between Sognefjord and Nordfjord lies the might Jostedal Glacier, stretching for 100 km (60 miles), the largest ice sheet in mainland Europe and a reminder of the great glaciers that carved out the fjords in the distant past. One of its arms is the Briksdal Glacier, a favourite tourist outing from Nordfjord, where visitors are taken to the foot of the glacier, a beauteous cascade of blue ice plunging into a clear lake.

Further north is the narrow and mysterious Geirangerfjord, which offers some of the most exciting fjord and mountain scenery in the country. Thin veils of water stream down sheer rock walls, among them the Bridal Veil and the Seven Sisters, which forms seven separate falls when it is swollen by melting ice in spring. The little village of Geiranger nestles at the head of the fjord, reached by a road that corkscrews 1,000 m (3,280 ft) down the mountain.

THE BLACK FOREST

The Romans called it the Hercynian Forest and left it undisturbed; in AD 363 the Emperor Julian referred to it as an 'impenetrable wilderness'. Though by the 16th century some areas around the river valleys had been cleared for villages and for agriculture, the forest itself was still considered a threatening, fearsome place, its dark heights mysterious and menacing. It was not until well into the 19th century that the Black Forest – it took its name back in the 8th century from its dense sweeps of pine trees – was recognized as a prime destination for holidays and health cures.

The Black Forest, or Schwarzwald, stretches for about 160 km (100 miles) from north to south, where it is bordered by the Rhine, and its width from east to west varies between 30 and 60 km (19 and 37 miles). It covers a gentle range of mountains, their heights rounded, their ridges flat-topped. The highest summits are Feldberg and Belchen in the south, both over 1,400 m (4,600 ft). Steep forests interspersed with narrow valleys clothe their western faces, while in the east lush green valleys widen out between gently rolling hills.

The forest at its blackest and most imposing can be seen from the Black Forest Highway (Schwarzwaldhochstrasse), running for 60 km (37 miles) along a mountain crest from Baden-Baden to Freudenstadt. There are no towns along this magnificent road but there plenty of stopping places for views across ridge after ridge of fir-clad hills, their lower slopes swathed in mist, occasionally opening out to a panoramic view of the Rhine plain below and the Vosges mountains beyond. The road passes the 17 m (56 ft) deep Mummelsee, the legendary home of water-nymphs and a picturesque, seven-stage waterfall at Allerheiligen. Nearby are the remains of a monastery that was founded in 1196 and rebuilt after being struck by lightning in 1470 and again in 1555. The third time lightning struck, in 1803, it was allowed to remain in ruins. Other famous routes are the Valley Road (Tälerstrasse) which runs through the deep gorge of the Murgtal, passing villages with old walls and half-timbered houses, romantic lakes and nature reserves, and the Hell Valley (Höllental) between Freiburg and Donaueschingen. The Hell Valley probably took its name from the difficult and dangerous mountain pass negotiated by travellers before the first road was specially built for Marie-Antoinette, bride of Louis XVI, for her journey to France in 1770. Brigands once hid in the rocks here to ambush unwary travellers, but now a broad highway sweeps through the valley. At the entrance, high upon a rock, is the bronze statue of a stag. The spot is called Hirschsprung, commemorating a fantastic leap across the valley by a stag pursued by huntsmen. On the way is Titisee, a 40 m (131 ft) deep lake in a former glacial valley, now a busy holiday centre.

It was the spas that first drew visitors to the region, the health-giving watering places on the edge of the forest itself. Badenweiler was already popular as a spa in the 1st century AD and has a well-preserved Roman bath. Wildbad was founded in the 14th century; legend says that it was discovered by a hunter who had wounded a wild boar and found it bathing in the healing spring, which has a temperature of up to 40°C (104°F). The king of the spas, however, is Baden-Baden, first developed by the Romans, and still famous for its curative springs, the warmest in Europe.

However charming the resorts and lakes of the Black Forest may be, its true glory is its trees, but in recent years there has been a growing threat to their survival. The problem began in the 1970s with the silver firs – the original Christmas trees – in the heights of the forest near Baden-Baden. The foliage of many of the firs turned brown, the needles fell and the trees died. At first this was put down to the effects of drought, which was particularly severe in 1976. Then the Norway spruce and beech trees also began to suffer. The damage spread so fast that by 1985 half of all Germany's trees were affected, one fifth of them seriously. Trees in the Black Forest have died in their thousands while scientists have debated and argued over the causes of decline, which has since been experienced in other countries, including Britain. In spite of strenuous opposition from some quarters, investigations have led inexorably to the conclusion that air pollutants, chiefly acid rain, have played a major role in depleting the forests. Though some steps have been taken to cut down on the burning of fossil fuels, the main cause of acid rain, 'green' supporters insist that far more dramatic measures will be necessary if the forest is to survive to delight future generations.

ASIA

Glacial lake on Baturo Glacier, Karakoram

THE HIMALAYAS

More than 30 of the mountain peaks of the 'Abode of Snow', the Himalayas, reach 7,300 m (24,000 ft) or more above sea level. They were thrown up from the ocean floor some 50 millions years ago after a collision between two of the great plates that form the earth's crust. The more southerly plate, bearing India and Australia, smashed into the Eurasian plate carrying Europe, Central Asia and China, cracking up the floor of an ancient sea and heaving it high into the air. Then, millions of years of storms, ice and snow shaped the mountains into their present form. The fossilized remains of sea creatures are found 6,000 m (20,000 ft) above sea level in the highlands of Tibet, where the land has been shielded from the full force of the weather.

The 2,400 km (1,500 miles) of the Himalayas stretch in a broad arc from Kashmir in the west to Bhutan in the east. Instead of an unbroken chain they form a series of roughly parallel ridges. The lowest and most southerly of the three main mountain ranges are the Siwaliks, comparatively low hills rising up to 914 m (3,000 ft) from the plain, seen in Hindu mythology as the roof's edge of the Himalayan home of Shiva, the destroyer. Next come the Lesser Himalayas, about 97 km (60 miles) wide, with an average height of 4,572 m (15,000 ft). The most northerly are the Greater Himalayas, with nine of the 14 highest peaks in the world. King of them all is Mount Everest (*see overleaf*) at 8,848 m (29,028 ft). Among the other awe-inspiring peaks are Kangchenjunga, 8,579 m (28,146 ft) on the Sikkim/Nepal frontier, seen in all its magnificence in the famous view from Darjeeling (*see right*), and Annapurna, 8,075 m (26,493 ft) in central Nepal. One of the world's most spectacular national parks is Sagarmatha, which includes the great trio of peaks – Everest with its companions Nuptse and Lhotse – as well as handsome peaks such as Mount Pumori.

Above the 6,400 m (21,000 ft) contour line the snow driven on to the mountains never melts, except close to the mountain ridges warmed by the sun. Between the ridges the snow is compacted into ice, which fractures and grinds its way down the mountain sides to form glaciers in the valleys enclosed by the mountains. It is here that the mighty rivers of the Indian subcontinent rise, the Indus, the Sutlej the Jumna, the Ganges and the Brahmaputra.

The first recognizable map of the Himalayas was drawn up by Father Antonio Monserrate, a member of the Spanish Jesuit mission to Akbar's court in 1579. The first Europeans to cross the range seem to have been two Portuguese priests, Father Antonio de Andrade and Brother Manuel Marques, who were investigating reports of a Christian settlement in Tibet in 1624. Other missionaries followed and made attempts at mapping the region; their findings, inaccurate as they were, were published as an atlas in the mid-18th century. It was not until the 1840s that the Survey of India began a systematic investigation of the region, estimating the height of the peaks. By 1862 more than 40 peaks of above 5,500 m (18,000 ft) had been climbed and surveyed.

The climate of the Himalayas varies widely, according to situation and altitude. For instance, the average minimum May temperature for Darjeeling at 1,945 m (6,380 ft) is 11°C (52°F) while at 4,877 m (16,000 ft) in the Everest region it will be more like −21°C (−7°F). the temperature and vegetation obviously dictate the animal life of the mountains. Elephants and rhinoceros are found in some areas of the low hills, though the Indian rhinoceros, once plentiful in the Outer Himalayas, is now almost extinct. In the forested areas live Himalayan black bear, Asian monkeys and goat antelopes, while beyond the tree line there is an occasional Tibetan yak, brown bear and snow leopard. The highest inhabitants are the Everest spiders, first discovered in 1924, living among the rocks at 6,500 m (21,325 ft).

The mountain Sherpas have always believed in the strange ape-like creature called the Yeti, nicknamed the Abominable Snowman and standing up to 3.6 m (12 ft) high. Sightings by European climbers in the first half of the 20th century were dismissed as figments of the imagination and the Yeti scalps produced by Sherpas were dismissed as fakes. Then in 1951 Eric Shipton was climbing with two other mountaineers in an unexplored area 40 to 65 km (30 to 40 miles) west of Everest when they came across a series of enormous footprints on a glacier. Shipton took photographs and, in spite of attempts to explain away the footprints as tracks of known animals, distorted by snow, they remain one of the best pieces of hard evidence for the existence of the Yeti.

MOUNT EVEREST

In the mid-19th century the highest peaks of the Himalayas lay beyond the reach of the surveyors who attempted to calculate their heights and it was not until 1852 that No XV was identified as the world's highest mountain. It straddled the border between Nepal and Tibet and already had two names; the Tibetans called it Chomolungma, meaning 'Goddess of the Universe' and the Nepalese knew it as Sagarmatha, in honour of the revered Sagar of Hindu mythology, the slayer of demons. The Survey of India called it Mount Everest, after Sir George Everest, surveyor-general in India in 1830–43. At the time they estimated its height at 8,840 m (29,002 ft), a mere 8 m (26 ft) short of the height officially accepted today.

Though the highest point on earth was an obvious target for climbers from all nations, Tibet and Nepal were closed to visitors until 1920, when the Tibetan government agreed to allow a British expedition to attempt the mountain. Between 1921 and 1938 there were seven major British assults on the summit. The most famous of these was in 1924 when two climbers, George Leigh Mallory and Andrew Irvine, disappeared into the mist while climbing the North Ridge and were never seen again. It was Mallory, a member of the first-ever expedition, who coined the classic reply when asked why he wanted to scale Everest: 'Because it's there'. The bodies of the two men were never found. No one knows what happened to them and there have been arguments ever since over whether or not they might have reached the summit.

With the ending of World War II, a number of countries joined the race to climb the so far unconquered Everest. In the early 1950s the Chinese invasion of Tibet meant that the border was closed once more and the northern approach to the mountain was no longer possible. Soon afterwards the government of Nepal was persuaded to admit mountaineers from other countries. This meant climbing the southern side of Everest, passing the treacherous Ice Fall that descends 600 m (1,969 ft) from the Western Cwm, then climbing the steep Lhotse face to reach the South Col. On the plus side, the southern route was better protected from gales and the final climb to the summit from the South Col was less steep than the last stretch on the northern side.

In 1952, Swiss climbers made two strong attempts at reaching the summit by the southern route. However, the mountain was finally conquered on 29 May 1953, when Edmund Hillary and Sherpa Tenzing Norgay finally stood on the summit. Hillary, a 33-year-old New Zealander, and his Nepalese Sherpa guide were members of a British expedition led by Sir John Hunt, which left Kathmandu on 10 March, Hunt's strategy was to set up a series of camps, with fewer members the higher the camp. The base camp was set up at the foot of the Ice Fall on 12 April, and within the next 10 days the second and third camps were established, bringing the expedition to the top of the Ice Fall at 6,096 m (20,000 ft). It was from the eighth camp, on the South Col, that the first assault on the summit was made by Tom Bourdillon and Charles Evans on 26 May, but lack of sufficient oxygen forced them to return. After being delayed by two days of gale-force winds, Hillary and Tenzing began their attempt at 6.30 am and reached the summit five hours later. Hillary was knighted for his achievement a few months later.

Apart from Sir Edmund Hillary, the most famous of Everest's mountaineers is Reinhold Messner, a former teacher from Italy. Up to 1978 it was believed that the thin air at such an altitude made it impossible to scale Everest without the help of bottled oxygen, but Messner and his companion, the Austrian Peter Habeler, managed to disprove the theory by climbing without supplementary oxygen. In 1980, Messner made the first solo ascent, still without extra oxygen. By 1986 he had become the first person to climb all 14 of the mountains with an altitude of 8,000 m (26,247 ft) or more. He scaled them without the use of extra oxygen.

Since the first ascent, many more 'firsts' have been achieved on the mountain. In 1965 the Indian Nawang Gombu Sherpa became the first person to succeed in climbing Everest twice. In 1975 Mrs Junko Tabei of Japan was the first woman to reach the top and in 1988 two expeditions reached the top from opposite sides for the first time.

Over 300 people have climbed Everest since 1953. However, according to Buddhist legend, the very first to arrive at the summit of the Goddess of the Universe was the 8th century guru who brought Buddhism to Tibet and who was carried in triumph up the mountain by the rays of the rising sun.

KARAKORAM

The Karakoram Range, which stretches for roughly 480 km (300 miles) through the disputed northern border territory of India and Pakistan, is known as 'The Roof of the World'. Its average height is around 6,100 m (20,000 ft) and 33 of its peaks rise above 7,300 m (23,950 ft). Among them is K2, the second highest mountain in the world at 8,610 m (28,248 ft). Karakoram means 'moving rock' and this is a dramatic and dangerous region, with the ever-present threat of avalanches, earthquakes and mudslides. Blizzards of 150 km/h (93 miles an hour) blast the peaks and melting glaciers cause serious flooding.

This is the most heavily glaciated range outside the polar regions; on the southern slope glaciers begin at 2,877 m (9,440 ft) and on the northern slopes at 3,530 m (11,580 ft). The Baltoro glacier runs 60 km (37 miles) from its beginning at the foot of K2 to eastern Baltistan. The Siachan, also from K2, runs for over 70 km (43 miles) and the Batura to the north stretches for 65 km (40 miles).

Eleven mountain passes cross the range but most are open only for a short time in summer. Though it seems almost incredible that human beings would be able to live a normal life in the harsh conditions, some tens of thousands of people actually do live here, in villages as high as 4,420 m (14,500 ft), and some nomadic groups herd yaks and goats on the mountain slopes. The ancient inhabitants of the region drew pictures of the ibex, once plentiful, but their numbers were drastically reduced by hunting. The mountains are still home to mountain sheep, wolf, Tibetan antelope and brown bear and they are one of the last refuges of the rare snow leopard.

In the first half of the 19th century, intrepid European climbers began to penetrate the Karakorams. The first to see the full grandeur of the panorama was Godfrey Thomas Vigne, who was overcome by the 'surpassig grandeur' of the 'vast assemblage of enormous summits'. The surveyors came next and in 1861 Colonel Henry Haversham Godwin-Austen, one of the greatest mountaineers of his day, explored some of the glaciers, attempting to sketch their course. In 1888, at a meeting of the Royal Geographical Society in London, it was proposed to name K2 after this early investigator but there was opposition to this because Godwin-Austen had not discovered the

mountain. So it has remained as K2. However, one of its glaciers bears his name, and one of the best known views of K2 is from the natural amphitheatre of Concordia, as it rises above Godwin-Austen Glacier.

The next major milestone came when Colonel Francis Younghusband crossed the Great Karakoram range by the Muztagh Pass, until then a completely unknown route. Younghusband was the first European to see the northern face of K2. In 1892 Sir William Martin Conway, later Lord Conway of Allington, led a party of mountaineers up the major glaciers, making a detailed reconnaissance map of his journey. He climbed Crystal Peak at 5,913 m (19,400 ft) and Pioneer Peak at 6,888 m (22,600 ft) but did not attempt K2, finding its majesty 'almost too brilliant for the eye to rest upon in its mantle of sunlit white. It was clear from base to summit, a broad and heavy mass, four-faced and four-ridged like the Great Pyramid.... Here for me the glory of this transcendent scenery culminated.'

Dr T.G. Longstaff made a major contribution to the knowledge of the region with his expedition across the Saltoro Pass, its existence previously only rumoured, reaching the Siachen glacier and discov-

ering a group of peaks they named Teram Kangri, the highest of them 7,464 m (24,489) ft). In the same year an Italian group led by the Duke of Abruzzi made two attempts on K2 but, though he managed to reconnoitre all four ridges, he had to give up at 6,706 m (22,000 ft) on the southern side and at 6,666 m (21,870 ft) on the north-west ridge. After weeks of pioneering effort he was forced to conclude that K2 was unclimbable.

A number of successive expeditions tried and failed. There were great hopes for the experienced American party of 1953 led by Dr Charles Houston but they were defeated by raging storms, and then one of the group developed phlebitis. Though there was a valiant attempt to drag him down the mountain on a stretcher, he was swept away in an avalanche and five other climbers almost died in a fall. The mountain was conquered only in 1954 by an Italian expedition under geologist Ardito Desio, with 11 climbers and 6 scientists. Achille Compagnoni and Lino Lacedelli scaled the summit from the last of several camps pitched at 8,230 m (27,000 ft), though they were forced to descend after dark. Even now, many of Karakoram's peaks have yet to be climbed.

THE HUNZA VALLEY

The author James Hilton drew the inspiration for his idyllic valley of Shangri-La in *Lost Horizon* – the beautiful, forgotten corner of the world where the people remained forever young – from the Hunza valley. Enclosed in the magnificent mountains of northern Pakistan the 2,440 m (8,000 ft) high valley was, until recently, more or less out cut off from civilization with a journey of 105 km (65 miles) taking three days. It is a scene of breathtaking beauty, carved by the glacier-fed torrent of the Hunza river and dominated by the single sharp peak of Mount Rakaposhi, its snowy summit rising 7,788 m (25,551 ft) above sea level. The mountaineer Eric Shipton described it as 'the ultimate manifestation of mountain grandeur'.

Hunza became part of Pakistan in 1974; before that it had been ruled for centuries by the same family. Even today, though the 30,000 inhabitants no longer pay regular taxes in kind to the Amir, most still regard him as their leader. Historians have never been able to offer proof of the ancestry of the Hunza people, though many theories have been advanced. One story is that, during the retreat of Alexander the Great's army, five of his soldiers caught a fever and were obliged to stay behind. Enchanted with the country, they stayed on and founded the various tribes of the area. However, the language of the Hunza, Burushaski, seems to bear no resemblance to any other existing language, so the mystery remains.

Through Hunza runs the famous 'Silk Route', the hazardous mountain track along which ancient traders brought their wares from China by packhorse, and for centuries the people of the valley carried out profitable raids on the caravans, ambushing them in the high passes and carrying off the ill-gotten gains. On the rocks above the village of Ganesh is the 'guest book of the Silk Road', where travellers have carved inscriptions, dates and names going back to the 5th century. In the 1880s Britain became concerned about a possible threat to the northern borders of the empire from the Russians and set up an outpost in Gilgit, to the south-west. The long-running conflict between Gilgit and Hunza led to a fierce battle between the British forces and the Hunza inhabitants, ending with the British capture of Baltit Fort, perched high above the valley. When Partition came in 1947, the northern region became part of Kashmir but this caused much ill-feeling among the mainly Muslim population and the region was eventually transferred to Pakistan.

The modern Hunza people live much the same way they have always lived, farming the neatly terraced fields and orchards that climb the steep cliffs and using both animal and human waste as the main fertilizer. Their main crops are barley and wheat, apricots, apples and pears. Though they do grow old, unlike James Hilton's characters, the inhabitants are long-lived; they claim that they have many centenarians still putting in a hard day's work on the land. Studies indicate that the mineral-rich drinking water, freedom from any modern stress and the low-fat, high-fibre diet all help to prolong life. Dried apricots, 20 varieties of them, are one of the chief foods. Apricots are used in cooking, field workers keep a pocket-full and nibble at them constantly during the day to keep up their energy, and the kernels are made into flour and oil for frying.

The small houses are built of undressed stone, with wooden verandahs on which the apricots are dried. They often form little groups, surrounded by a protective wall, a layout dating from the days of skirmishes between rival kingdoms. The religion is Ismaili, a progressive sect led by the Aga Khan. The local dress is a long shirt worn over baggy trousers, with woollen beret with rolled edges for the men and an embroidered cap for the women.

The 400-year-old Baltit Fort still stands guard over the Hunza capital Karimabad and until 1960 it was home of the Amir. From the roof there is a superb view out across the valley. Behind the fort, among a cluster of peaks, is a thin, dark column, on which snow cannot settle for long. It is named for the legendary Princess Bubuli, who was left behind on the mountain when her husband went off to war. When the wind whips round the peak, her weeping can be heard throughout the valley.

The Karakoram Highway, which links Pakistan to China along the roads that rise to 4,877 m (16,000 ft), is a remarkable engineering feat said to have cost the life of one worker for every kilometre. When its was built in the 1980s it ended Hunza's isolation for ever. In time the Hunza lifestyle and diet may change, threatening the tranquility of the region and the longevity of its inhabitants.

DEAD SEA

The Dead Sea is not in fact a sea at all but a landlocked lake, the lowest body of water on earth – and the saltiest. It stands 402 m (1,320 ft) below sea level and, at its deepest point, its waters descend another 395 m (1,296 ft). The lake is eight times as salty as the Mediterranean, the Pacific or the Atlantic. Nearly a quarter of its volume is made up of dissolved solids, mostly common salt, but there are also high concentrations of magnesium chloride, potassium, calcium and iodine. The water is so buoyant that is impossible to sink; it is also impossible to tread water, dive or swim. Bathers are advised to lean back gradually into the cradling water (otherwise they are likely to flip over like corks) and they can float completely horizontal.

Though the Jordan River and a number of springs and streams pour 4 million tonnes of fresh water into the Dead Sea every day, it evaporates so fast in the searing sun that it has no chance to dilute the thick, salty lake. The evaporation process leaves a constant haze above the waters which, together with the complete stillness, gives the Dead Sea its air of utter tranquility. Temperatures can reach 55°C (131°F) in this sheltered spot and the level of the lake is falling all the time; there are plans to restore it by cutting a channel through from the Mediterranean.

In the Middle Ages, the belief was that no birds flew over the Dead Sea because the air was full of poisonous vapours. The real reason for the lack of birds is that there is no food. Any fish borne in along the rivers would be unable to survive the salt; and instead of vegetation round the edge, salt columns (*see inset*) rise above the water like baby icebergs. For humans, however, the atmosphere is healthy, the air is rich in oxygen, good for respiratory complaints, and the water is said to be helpful in curing skin ailments. Most visitors experiment by smearing themselves from head to foot with the famous black mud, which is supposed to have a rejuvenating effect. Skin-care products, which use the mud as their base, are on sale locally.

The Dead Sea forms part of the border between Israel and Jordan,

with the white limestone walls of the Plain of Moab rising to the east and the Plateau of Judaea to the west. Tradition says that the remains of Sodom and Gommorah, the biblical cities destroyed by fire as a punishment for their godless inhabitants, lie at the bottom of the lake. The book of Genesis tells the story of Abraham's nephew Lot who was allowed to escape with his family, on condition that they did not look back. Lot's wife could not resist a glance over her shoulder and was turned into a pillar of salt. She still stands at the south-western end of the lake – one of a number of salt hillocks.

In a cave in the Qumran Valley, on the north-west shore, a Bedouin shepherd boy searching for a lost sheep in 1947 found some earthenware jars containing what he imagined to be pieces of old leather. He sold them to a cobbler but they were subsequently identified as ancient manuscripts. These were the first Dead Sea Scrolls, containing sections of the Old Testament. Later many more scrolls were discovered, the earliest known manuscripts of the Bible. These valuable additions to biblical scholarship are thought to have belonged to the library of a Jewish sect, the Essenes, who lived in the area from about 100 BC to AD 70.

Further south is the oasis of En Gedi where, according to the Book of Samuel, David hid to escape Saul's anger. The natural springs trickling down the mountain slopes produce a completely different environment from the arid lake shore. There is a kibbutz and a nature reserve, and the deep mountain canyon has a luxuriant plant growth, many species of butterflies, and herds of wild ibex.

The most historically significant Dead Sea site is Masada, perched on a 457 m (1,500 ft) mountain plateau, and this is accessible by cable-car. This was originally Herod's fortress, where he could be certain of safety for himself and his family. Later it passed into Roman hands but in AD 66 a group of Jewish zealots, in revolt against Rome, overpowered the garrison, which became a stronghold for all rebels escaping after the collapse of the rebellion and the fall of Jerusalem in AD 70. Masada held out for another three years and seemed impregnable until Flavius Silva, commanding the 10th Legion, decided to build a ramp up the west side of the mountain. According to the historian Josephus, the leader of the Jews exhorted them to die rather than become slaves and mass suicide of the fortress's inhabitants followed.

CAPPADOCIA

The eerie moonscape of cones, pyramids and chimneys nestling in the valleys of Cappadocia in central Turkey had its beginings with an explosion of the volcano Erciyas Dagi, between Kayseri and Develi around 3 million years ago. The eruption spread thick layers of ash and lava over the surrounding area, the ash turning into soft white rock known as tufa, while the lava hardened into black basalt. Over thousands of years, as the climate changed to give wetter and cooler conditions, water cut gorges in the soft tufa. Natural erosion teased away at the sides of the gorges, seeking out any weakness, until the masses left standing were those topped by the more resilient volcanic rock. The result is the myriad cones with caps of stone, known as 'fairy chimneys'. Many are coloured in bands of red and ochre caused by the minerals within the rock. Local legend, however, has a different version of the origin of the cones: the story goes that when the people of the valley were attacked by the army of a land-hungry king, they prayed to Allah for deliverance and he answered their prayer by turning the hostile soldiers to stone so that they stand rooted to the spot for all eternity.

No one knows how early in the Christian period hermits began to make their simple cells in Cappadocia but there were certainly small settlements of monks here by the 4th century. They found it easy to cut through the tufa to make dwellings or chapels. Between the 5th and the 9th centuries their numbers were swelled by a major influx of refugees, fleeing from religious persecution in Anatolia.

Overall several centuries, hundreds of rock churches were carved out, designed on the same principles as their stone counterparts in the Byzantine style with domes, apses, naves and aisles decorated with frescoes that remain remarkably fresh and colourful to this day. Some were decorated in the iconoclastic period, when it was not permitted to use pictures of God or Christ in human form, and during this time the decorations were likely to be geometric patterns, or symbols such as crosses and fish. In 842 the iconoclastic controversy was finally resolved and the religious painters could once more give their imagination full reign. Many covered the walls of their churches with scenes from Old and New Testaments.

One of the most impressive collections of churches is in the valley of Göreme, where a dozen richly decorated rock caves only metres apart jostle for attention. The largest is Tokali Kilise, the 'Church with the Shield', hollowed out of a rock pillar, with paintings in reds, yellows and greens, recording the life of Jesus and his disciples in chronological order. St Michael, St George and St Basil also appear in the frescoes, which date from the 10th century. Karanlik Kilise, the 'Dark Church', portrays instantly recognizable scenes: the Crucifixion and the Last Supper, where a huge fish is set out on a dish ready for the meal, stand out. The Byzantine emperor Constantine and his wife Helena are depicted in Yilanli Kilise, the 'Snake Church', and the Carikli Kilise, the 'Sandal Church', is so called because, below the scene of the ascension, are footprints copied exactly from those in the Church of the Ascension in Jerusalem.

As well as chapels, whole monasteries were created and can be seen complete with kitchens, cells and refectories with carved stone benches. One of the oldest is at Cemil in the Gorgoli valley, which includes the 7th century church of St Stephen with its horseshoe apse and the church of St Michael with 11th century paintings. The monastery at Acik Sariya, the 'open palace', is built on several levels underground, its construction made possible by the specially soft tufa of the area. The decorations here are reliefs, not paintings, and include two bulls facing one another angrily, apparently raring for a fight.

The valleys here are unexpectedly luxuriant, with pigeon droppings providing useful fertilizer, and over the centuries since the Christian colonization many thousands of people have found shelter among the rocks. At Ortahisar the modern village huddles round an enormous rock needle peppered with troglodyte dwellings. The rock at Uchisar was turned into a massive fortress, and once housed as many as 1,000 people; it has scores of rooms and is dotted with windows like a Swiss cheese.

In the valley of Zelve, scholars have only recently been able to explore all the ancient religious settlements, for the caves were still fully occupied until 1950 when they were declared unsafe and the villagers were relocated. The little rock dwellings were remarkably cosy, keeping out both the winter cold and summer heat. Nowadays they are more likely to be used as storerooms to preserve locally grown fruit for long periods.

PAMUKKALE

The 100 basins of Pamukkale, set in dazzling white cliffs, hold innumerable mineral-laden pools that have the reputation for soothing nerves, lowering blood pressure, easing rheumatism and treating heart disease as well as eye and skin disorders. Looking like a great stone waterfall, scalloped terraces stand 100 m (328 ft) on the side of Cal Dagi mountain in western Anatolia, Turkey, standing out against the dark background of pine trees.

Pamukkale means 'cotton castle' and there are several theories about how it came by the name. One is that the water was specially good for washing sheep's wool, another is that the name comes from the 12th century fortress that once stood here, though only a few stones remain at the top of the cliff. Local legend says that this is the place where ancient giants used to dry their cotton crops.

The thermal spring bubbles from the ground at 37°C (98.5°F), bringing with it a large amount of calcium carbonate. As the water cools in the air the calcium carbonate is deposited, fresh layers all the time, to build up basins, linked by calcified waterfalls. Other minerals, like magnesium and iron, are contained in the water and this creates shades of yellow and brown to highlight the white. Each year the water leaves sufficient new layers of calcium carbonate to protect the 'cotton castle' from the effects of erosion by weathering, though air pollution from increased motor traffic threatens to turn the brilliant white of the terraces into a dull grey.

The healing powers of the Pamukkale spring have been famous for thousands of years. King Eumones of Pergamon founded the city of Hierapolis here in 190 BC, naming it for Hiera, wife of Telephos, the legendary founder of Pergamon; but when the Romans took over in 133 BC, they thought the name meant Holy City. Under the Romans, Hierapolis became a popular watering place, favoured by a string of emperors. However, frequent earthquakes in the region meant much repair and reconstruction; in the time of Nero the city was so badly damaged that he had it completely rebuilt.

The bathhouse, now a museum displaying statuary and other site finds, dates from the 2nd century AD and includes calderium and frigidarium, a large gymnasium and a private bathroom for the emperor. The theatre, impressively set on the hillside, has an auditorium with 50 rows of seats and an imperial box.

Alongside the ruined Temple of Apollo, with its Corinthian columns, is the Plutonium, sacred to Pluto, the god of the underworld. The sacred sites of the two gods were placed side by side so that their light and dark powers could balance out one another. A cave in the rock inside the temple gives off a strong and unpleasant smell from the narrow opening. The Greek geographer Strabo, when he visited this strange spot 2000 years ago, described it as follows: 'Outside the enclosure the air is free of fumes when the wind is not blowing and it is possible to approach quite close; but for any living creature that enters, death is instantaneous. Bulls taken in, for example, collapse and die. We ourselves sent in some little birds which at once fell lifeless.' The fumes come from a hot spring within the cave but in ancient times it was thought that they showed the presence of evil spirits and eunuch priests were kept as guards at the entrance. According to Strabo these eunuchs were the only living creatures who were not affected by the fumes, able to go into the cave without even holding their breath, and they never came to any harm.

The necropolis at Hierapolis is the largest in this part of the world. Some of the 1,200 tombs stand solid and proud on the hillsides, others lie broken and lidless. There are tombs like small temples, the 'houses of the dead'; others have vaulted underground chambers; yet others have an enormous sarcophagus mounted on a high pedestal. The imposing nature of the tombs bears witness to the number of wealthy Romans who came in search of the curative powers of the water without success.

Just beyond the city walls is an important Christian building: the octagonal Martyrium of St Philip the Apostle. This dates from the 5th century and was erected to honour the martyred saint who had retired to Hierapolis.

Excavations at Pamukkale were begun by the German expert Carl Humann in 1887, and from the 1950s onwards Italian archaeologists have explored the area. Now that it has become a popular tourist destination, one motel has the top basin of the cotton castle as its swimming pool so that bathers can swim right to the edge of the cliff and look over the plain of Denizli. At another, visitors can bathe on the site of the sacred spring, among broken marble columns.

LAKE BAIKAL

An old Russian song calls Lake Baikal, its crescent shape extending 650 km (400 miles) through south-eastern Siberia, a 'majestic ocean'. It is the seventh largest lake in the world but its depth, rather than its size, is its main claim to fame. It is the deepest lake on earth, with an average depth of 730 m (2,395 ft), but sinking as deep as 1,620 m (5,314 ft) in places. It contains as much water as all the Great Lakes in North America put together; in all, one fifth of the world's freshwater reserves.

Baikal was formed 250 million yers ago and the origin of its name has remained a mystery; one theory is that it comes from the Mongolian 'Bai-Gal' meaning 'big fire', another that it comes from the Turkish 'Baikul', meaning 'rich lake'. The waters, so clear that it is possible to see 40 m (130 ft) below the surface, never warm thoroughly in summer, with the surface water temperature near the banks sometimes twice as high as the temperature further out across the lake. In winter the lake stays frozen for four to five months by which time the ice can reach 110 cm (43 in) thick. However, deep within the lake the temperature stays at about 3.5℃ (38°F).

The lake is fed by 336 rivers and streams, the largest being the Selenga, which is 1,480 km (920 miles) long and supplies half Baikal's total inflow. It is drained only by the Angara, which joins the Yenisei. Legend tells that old Baikal had 366 quiet obedient daughters, and one rebel, Angara, who defied her father to elope with her lover Yenisei. As they fled the old man's wrath, the furious Baikal hurled a large boulder after them; this is the Shaman Stone which stands at the spot where Angara leaves the lake.

The age and depth of Lake Baikal provides a unique habitat and the plants and animals here have been isolated so long that they have developed quite differently from those in other waters. Out of more than 1,800 different types of plants and animals identified at Baikal, at least 1,000 of them are unique to the region. Most of these species have developed in deep water, where conditions remain fairly constant. Round the shoreline, however, where conditions are more likely to vary with the seasons, most of the plants and animals to be found also occur in other areas of Europe and Asia.

One third of all identified species of freshwater shrimps in the world come from Lake Baikal and, in all, 255 species of shrimp are found here. These, evolving deep within the lake, are so pale as to be almost white. They have no pigment in their eyes and have developed long antennae for finding their way in the blackness of the water.

The *Comephorus baicalensis* and the *Comephorus dybowskii*, both species of fish to be found only in Baikal, are about 13 cm (7 in) long and completely transparent, living in water down to 500 m (1,640 ft) and feeding on shrimps and other tiny fish. Among the other 50 species of fish is the omul, which remains in deep water throughout the winter and then comes to feed in the shallower areas as the surface temperature warms with the coming of spring. Omuls often weight 450 g (1 lb) and make up two-thirds of the commercial fish catch from the lake.

The Baikal seal is another unique species, living mainly at the northern end of the lake and around one of the largest of its 27 islands, Ushkanii. This is a small, fresh-water seal with an average weight of around 100 kg (220 lb) which keeps alive in winter by gnawing breathing holes through the ice just like its Arctic relatives. The presence of the seals led local fishermen to believe in an underground tunnel which connected Lake Baikal to the Arctic Ocean. However, this theory has been disproved and scientists believe that the forerunners of the species must have reached the lake along the Yenisei and Angara rivers in the glacial period.

BEPPU

The Japanese islands are the summits of submarine mountains, many of them volcanic. At least 50 of these volcanoes are still active, so that minor eruptions and earthquakes are frequent and hot springs abound. Beppu, on the quiet southern island of Kyushu, is the most renowned of the *onsen*, or hot springs, areas, where well over 3,000 springs spurted from the ground following the eruption of Mount Tsurumi in AD 867. The volcanic peak of Tsurumi still stands 1,375 m (4,511 ft) above the bay. It is extinct now but many of the springs it created have been used as spas since the earliest times. Each spring produces several million cubic feet of water and bubbling pools and jets of steam emerge from all over the green hillsides. The ever-present reminder that beneath the security of the earth's crust there is a region of searing heat and molten rocks has led to the name *jigoku* (hell) for the springs of Beppu.

The most fascinating springs are the 'eight hells' on a 20 km (12 mile) circuit, all with different colours and temperatures, some spurting like explosive geysers, others bubbling gently through liquid mud. Local stallholders boil eggs in the waters to demonstrate the heat of the water. Chinoike-jigoku, the 'blood-pond hell' (*see left*), its deep-red colour coming from the underwater oxidation, is 165 m (541 ft) deep and holds a temperature of 93°C (199°F). It is renowned for its beneficial effect in treating skin complaints. The 120 m (395 ft) deep Umi-jigoku, the 'sea-hell', is just as hot as Chinoike-jigoku and has emerald-green waters and a fringe of tropical foliage. Kamado-jigoku's sizzling mud is milky-white and Bozu-jigoku's great spluttering grey bubbles heave and pop. Oniyama-jigoku, 'devil mountain', has alligator and crocodile breeding pools beside the springs.

All the springs contain the same elements – alkali, sulphur, carbon and iron – but the proportions vary. Sulphur-rich springs are said to be good for those with circulatory disorders while alkali springs can help those with skin complaints. Carbonic springs are supposed to help those suffering from stomach ailments. Japanese scientists take the beneficial effects of the waters very seriously and the University of Kyoto has set up an Institute of the Study of Hot Springs, while a special physical science laboratory is analysing the results of research at Beppu. Other laboratories carry out research into the geothermal activity of the area. Water piped from the springs is used to heat the many spa hotels and wells have been drilled to harness steam for use in generating electricity.

Some of the pools at Beppu can accommodate 1,000 people at a time; others have fanciful names like 'Dream Public Baths' and 'Flower Public Baths' and have lush garden settings. In addition to hot-water pools, mud baths and hot sand baths are very popular. Until the last decade, spas had fallen out of fashion in Japan and were patronized mainly by the elderly and the sick. Now the health-giving properties of mineral waters are back in vogue and spas like Beppu are crowded all year round. The tradition of public bathing in Japan contributes to their popularity; bathing has always been regarded as an important ritual, not simply for cleansing the body but as a way of ridding the mind of impurities and promoting a calm, relaxed mental attitude. Until the 1950s, men and women had always bathed together in the public bathhouses but pressure from female Members of Parliament and religious leaders led to the passing of a law which segregated the sexes. The continued mixed bathing at the spas may have contributed to the resurgence of interest. Though some of the *onsen* visitors are interested in the curative properties of the springs, most simply enjoy them for the relaxation they afford.

Beppu attracts millions of Japanese visitors a year to Kyushu, which is separated from the main island of Honshu by the Kammen Kaikyo strait, 700 m (2,297 ft) wide. Comparatively few Western visitors reach the island, though it lays claim to being the birthplace of Japanese civilization, the base from which the grandson of the sun-goddess Amaterasu ruled the whole country. His descendant Jimmu left Kyushu to become Japan's first emperor and founded the line that continues to modern times. Japan's first contact with the outside world also came through Kyushu, when Portuguese ships arrived in the 16th century. The Spanish, the English and the Dutch followed, but rivalries caused problems and from 1637 Europeans were allowed to enter the country only through the single port of Nagasaki. This remained the only port open to the West until the mid-19th century, when Japan once more opened its doors to Western trade and influence.

THE YANGTZE GORGES

The shores of the Yangtze gorges in Sichuan province, China, are dotted with pagodas built to ensure safe passage for travellers, propitiating the gods and warding off evil spirits. Modern steamers take 12 hours to pass through the three great gorges, but in the past this was a long and hazardous journey, with large boats having to be hauled upstream by parties of 'trackers' pulling on heavy ropes. One 80 tonne boat would need 300 of these men, and even then there were frequent wrecks.

The Chinese call the Yangtze river the Chang Jiang (Long River) and indeed it is the third longest river in the world, after the Nile and the Amazon. It rises in the Tanggula mountains of Tibet and runs for 6,300 km (3,915 miles) through Sichuan and Yunnan, across central China and into the East China Sea at Shanghai. For hundreds of years it has been China's life blood, its main line of communication. It still carries a wide variety of traffic; passenger steamers, great lumbering coal barges, sailing junks and long bamboo rafts propelled by oars at either end. The gorges are the most romantic of the river's sights, narrowing to 100 m (328 ft) in places and cradling the fierce river which swells by 30 m (100 ft) in the rainy season. They came into being some 70 million years ago after a major shift in the earth's crust had changed the position of two neighbouring mountain ranges. According to legend, they were created by the mythical emperor Yu the Great who hacked his way through the rock face to make a channel to drain off floods from Sichuan province.

The gorges are negotiated by passenger boats plying between Chongqing and Wuhan, and the whole journey takes three days and two nights. Boats starting from Chongqing, an industrial city at the confluence of the Jialing and Yangtze Rivers, pass the fascinating 18th century pagoda of Shibaozhai, 55 m (180 ft) high, on the way to the gorges. This began as a cliff-top Buddhist temple, where the piety of would-be worshippers was tested by the necessity of hauling themselves up the rocks by means of a chain. Later the twelve storeys of the pagoda were added to provide a more civilized

climb, each of them bearing the name of a famous Chinese general or writer. Two steep cliffs form a natural gateway to the first gorge, Qutang, which is the shortest and most dramatic and only 8 km (5 miles) long. Caves high in the steep rocks were once the burial places of warriors; coffins found have contained weapons and armour. A set of small holes running up the cliffside is said to be a staircase made by the bodyguard Meng Liang, who was seeking a secure burial place for his warrior master. Near the little town of Wushan visitors can take a side trip through the three 'little gorges', open to foreigners only since 1985.

Wuxia gorge (Sorcerer's gorge), 40 km (25 miles) long, is dominated by the 12 'Fairy Peaks', each with its own name. The story is that the Queen of Heaven sent a dozen of her helpers to assist in taming the waters at the time of creation and, when their task was complete, they were turned to stone so that they could remain and watch over travellers on the river. The Goddess Peak, 12 m (39 ft) high, is supposed to be Yao Ji, the youngest of the group. The peak is frequently obscured by mist; when Yao Ji's head can be seen clearly, it means good fortune for all who look on her. A dignatary from the 3rd century is supposed to have inscribed the six Chinese characters seen on the nearby rock, reading 'Wu Gorge boasts craggy cliffs'.

Xiling, the last of the gorges, is 80 km (50 miles) long and is actually made up of several smaller gorges with fanciful names like the Cow and Ox Liver Gorges, the Sword Gorge and the Military Book Gorge. The legend of the Empty Boat Gorge was that any boatman who did not throw all his cargo into the river at this point would go down with his craft. Myth was, to some exent, backed by fact: Xiling was the most dangerous of the gorges, with projecting rocks and powerful rapids, and right up until the 1950s boat passengers had to disembark and make their way along a mountain track to avoid the worst of the gnashing waters. The White Bone Pagoda on the cliff is the last resting place for the bones of those who drowned here.

Towards the end of Xiling the orange trees dotting the hills give way to sandstone quarries and the boat emerges from the gorges and through the locks of the huge Gezhouba Dam with its 27 floodgates.

GUILIN

The Chinese of Guangxi-Zhuang province have always believed that Guilin was the most beautiful place in the world. Young lovers knew it as the most romantic of destinations for a honeymoon, long before it was opened up to the outside world as a tourist centre. Craggy hills rise suddenly from ground level, forming unexpected shapes and patterns, dotted through the town itself and spreading out through the surrounding countryside. The Li river winds through the landscape, reflecting peaks that are often swathed in mist (*see right*), providing a strange, other-worldly quality. There is a theory that the landscape of Guilin was the original inspiration for the unique style of Chinese painting; whether or not this is true, Chinese painters and poets have for centuries been using their talents to describe its beauty. The Tang dynasty poet Han Yu provided a lyrical description: 'the river is a torquoise gauze belt, the mountains a jade clasp.' The story goes that one poet was so lost for words when gazing at the scenery that he sat for years trying to compose a suitable verse and eventually turned to stone. He sits as a pillar of rock called the Old Scholar in the Reed Flute Cave.

Geologists, with a less poetic turn of mind, see this as one of the world's most impressive karst regions, where a 300 million-year old layer of sea-bed limestone was heaved above the water by violent movements in the earth's crust, then eroded into striking formations (*see below*) both above and below the ground in the same process that has created so many of the world's natural wonders.

Though the hills are not particularly high, like, for example, the 152 m (499 ft) Duxiu, the 'Peak of Solitary Beauty' which dominates Guilin, they rise so sharply that they seem like mountains. From the top of Duxiu there is a sublime view over the other peaks, especially at sunset, when they are bathed in pink and gold and purple. Some of the hills have been named for their shape: the Camel, the Climbing Tortoise, the Elephant Trunk, which resembles an elephant lowering its trunk to drink from the river, and the Folded Silk Hill, where several peaks rise closely behind one another. The peaks of Seven Star Park take their name fromt he star pattern of Ursa Major, the Big Dipper.

The hillsides are riddled with caves and many of them, like the Seven Star cave which has been a popular attraction for 1,500 years, are decorated with imaginatively lighted stalactites and stalagmites. The Reed Flute cave, which has been used over the centuries as a secret hiding place in time of trouble, was opened to the public only in 1958 and its formations are particularly vivid. At the foot of Crescent Hill is the Dragon Cave, full of tablets bearing the names of earlier visitors, some going back 800 years. It is named for the markings on the ceiling, patterned in the shape of a dragon attempting to escape. One of the most famous of the caverns is the Wind Cave, in the side of the Folded Silk Hill, which remains cool on the hottest days because a current of cold air constantly blows through it.

Guilin means 'forest of cassia' and the hundreds of thousands of cinnamon (cassia) trees that shade the streets fill the town with their scent in the flowering season, between August and October. The remains of a Ming palace, dating from the 1370s, stand at the foot of the Peak of Solitary Beauty; the founder of the Ming dynasty, Wong Hu, made the town the capital of the province. The most popular tourist attraction of Guangxi-Zhuang is the boat journey to Yangshuo, 80 km (50 miles) along the Li River. The scenery changes with every curve of the river – bamboo forests, paddy fields, overhanging rocks – everywhere there are the limestone tors, some smooth-topped, some jagged, some looking for all the world like a collection of hats, while others resemble galloping horses.

KRAKATOA

Until the late 19th century, Krakatoa was a little known island lying between the larger Indonesian islands of Java and Sumatra. In 1883, however, it took its place in the history books when its giant volcano came to life, causing one of the most catastrophic explosions the world has ever known. Before the eruption, Krakatoa was 9 km (5.5 miles) long, with a string of volcanic cones running from north to south, the highest of them 813 m (2,667 ft) above sea level.

No one expected dramatic activity from Krakatoa; the only record of a previous eruption was a modest explosion and a small lava flow in 1680. Some seismic activity began in the area in the autumn of 1880, with a succession of minor earthquakes over the next three years until 20 May 1883, when a series of volcanic explosions could be heard up to 160 km (100 miles) away. A great column of smoke and ash 11 km (7 miles) high rose from one of the minor craters, Perboewetan. As the first explosion died away there was a second and then a third. By the end of May there was a period of calm but in mid-June the explosions began again and by early August observers reported that three vents were in active eruption and a dozen more were showing signs of activity.

When the huge volcano Krakatoa itself came to life, on 26 August, the eruptions came so thick and fast that they merged into one continuous roar. On the morning of 27 August came four thunderous explosions, so powerful that Australians over 3,000 km (2,000 miles) away were woken by a rumble like rock-blasting and the noise was heard 4,800 km (3,000 miles) away on Rodriguez island in the Indian Ocean. The climax came at 10 am with the biggest bang in recorded history, when a column of fire rose 80 km (50 miles) into the air.

The islands themselves were uninhabited but the explosions triggered huge waves called *tsunamis*, rising to 38 m (125 ft) high and smashing over the coasts of Java and Sumatra, sweeping away 300 towns and villages and causing the death of 36,000 people. Corpses littered the sea and fields of pumice lay so thick on the water that would-be rescuers could walk across them. The air was so thick with ash that the surrounding area remained in darkness for two and a half days. The effects of the seismic sea waves were felt as far away as San Francisco and the English Channel, with unusually high tides recorded. Fine dust discharged into the upper atmosphere travelled right round the world and the effects were felt throughout the following year. There was a general cooling of temperatures as the volcanic dust blocked the sun's rays, and there were magnificent red sunsets throughout the Far East and as far afield as London and the west coast of America.

After the first great explosion, volcanic activity continued for 33 hours. When the ash-laden air eventually cleared, the mountain had disappeared and the othe small islands of the group were buried under such a thick layer of ash that nothing could grow there for five years. However, Krakatoa refused to die. Over the next four decades, roars and rumbles disturbed the calm of the sea where the volcano once stood, then in January 1925 a smoking volcanic cone emerged above the water. Several times over the following years it submerged and rose again, growing with periodic eruptions to its present size of 91 m (300 ft). It has been named Anak Krakatoa, 'Child of Krakatoa' (*right and inset*).

Studies of Krakatoa, which began while the rock was still smouldering, considerably advanced the science of vulcanology. Analysis of the ash and pumice revealed that only 10 per cent came from the ruined cone of the mountain; the rest came from the magma chamber within the volcano, indicating that volcanic cones were likely to collapse in on themselves, rather than being blown into the air, as had previously been believed.

PHANG NGA BAY

Phang Nga Bay, in southern Thailand, is a place of exquisite beauty, where a throng of limestone rocks rise from jade green waters, their sides dripping with tropical plants. Some are sheer-sided, rising several hundred metres, some loom as great humps, others look like upside-down mountains. For much of the year a heat haze blurs the edges of the scene, increasing the air of magical unreality.

Before the James Bond film *The Man with the Golden Gun* used Phang Nga Bay as one of its locations in 1974, it was silent and unvisited; now, however, it is a favourite tourist location. Long-tailed boats with rows of passengers, seated two-abreast, carve through the water, sending up curves of spray, following the route taken by James Bond (Roger Moore) when he raced across the bay to confront the villain Scaramanga (Christopher Lee) on his private island. The island's name, Khoa Ping Kan, means 'two islands leaning back to back', because an ancient earth tremor split the island down the middle so that the peaks of the two halves lean into one another. Today it is popularly known as the James Bond island, and though it is uninhabited, local vendors are there to meet the boats, selling pearls drawn from nearby bays. The photogenic Koh Tapu, the pillar of rock called the 'nail island', stands just off the shore.

The limestone rocks are honeycombed with caves, some dis-appearing into the darkness of the cliffs, others burrowing right through and emerging into the light at the other side. At Khao Kien ('painted mountain'), the walls are covered with primitive paintings of men, fish and animals. Hoh Kong is like a decorated stone room, and at Tham Lod the boat drifts along a tunnel right through the middle of one of the islands, where long, constantly dripping stalactites hang from the roof. At the mouth of the bay, like a dog sitting on guard, is the Pekinese Rock.

Two hundred years ago a small party of Muslims arrived in Phang Nga from Malaysia and set up their flag on one of the islands. The fishing village of Koh Pannyi ('flag island') has been there ever since, built out on stilts over the water, its rickety wooden pier sheltered beneath the rock, its tiny mosque clinging to the cliff face, with the minarets glinting.

The picturesque limestone formations that have brought fame to Phang Nga extend southwards along the magnificently scenic Anda-man coast to Krabi, where some of the stacks are whimsically named Bird, Cat and Mouse islands. Idyllic white sand beaches are fringed with palms and lapped by waters so clear that it is possible to see right down to the vivid rocks and corals below. At Ao Son beach, fishermen make offerings for safety at sea in the Princess Cave at the foot of the cliffs. Legend has it that a goddess who fell in love with a fisherman took human form for his sake and died here in childbirth. At the foot of the cliffs to the west of Krabi lies a collection of great rock slabs formed from compacted sea shells some 75 million years old, looking like tumbled gravestones – hence the gloomy name of Shell Cemetery.

About 40 km (25 miles) offshore is the dramatic uninhabited island of Phi Phi Le, its coast dotted with limestone pinnacles like guardian sentinels. The rock is pitted with dark caves and in one spot the sea has carved its way into an enclosed canyon where the water shines brilliant, translucent green. However, the main won-ders of Phi Phi Le are its highly prized birds' nests. Hundreds upon hundreds of swallows nest here, favouring the upper reaches of one particularly high cave. They weave their nests from threads of saliva which harden as they dry. When dissolved in chicken broth they make the famous Chinese birds' nest soup. The nests from Phi Phi Le are highly prized, both for their taste and their medicinal qualities.

THE GANGES

The Ganges is far more than just a river. It has a special place in the Hindu religion as it is claimed to be the goddess Ganga herself, ordered by the Lord Shiva, the destroyer and reproducer, to flow down from heaven to give immortal life to those whose ashes are covered by her waters. Ganga was so powerful that Shiva had to protect the earth by breaking her descent with his head. Ever afterwards she has flowed from the locks of his hair. To her people she is the great 'mother' river, her water the promise of salvation. Only when her followers have offended her does she unleash her force, overflowing her banks and causing widespread destruction. Jawaharlal Nehru summed up the feeling of the people of India for the beloved river 'round which are intertwined her racial memories, her hopes and fears, her songs of triumph, her victories and her defeats'.

The towns on the banks of the river are sanctified by their position and every major junction in the river's course is a famous pilgrimage site. Every devout Hindu longs to make the pilgrimage to the source of the river, in an ice cave at the foot of the Himalayan Gangotri glacier. Pilgrims bathe in the icy water and say prayers for their ancestors in the 200-year old temple, which stands at 3,000 m (10,000 ft) in superb mountain scenery. Holy men live as hermits in remote caves in the hillsides; some can be seen meditating beside the water, standing on one leg for an astonishingly long time or sitting naked on the bank, covered in ashes as a sign of penitence. Their hair is long and matted to demonstrate how little they care about physical things and their only possessions are a pot and wooden staff.

Allahabad, where the waters of the Jumna join those of the Ganges, and Hardwar, where the river passes through a gorge before beginning its winding course across the plains, are also important centres of worship, but the most holy city of all is Varanasi, the 'eternal city', a centre of learning for the past 2,000 years. At dawn hundreds – sometimes thousands – of pilgrims gather at the *ghats*, the steps leading down to the river, for a ritual dip, confident that

immersion in the water will cleanse them of all their sins. The purification ritual requires worshippers to bathe at each of five special *ghats* in the course of a day. Many old and sick people gather in the city, for the belief is that any Hindu who dies here will go straight to heaven without going through the long cycle of rebirth. For Hindus, burning the body is the means of releasing the soul and on the burning *ghats* fires burn constantly while corpses, (women wrapped in red cloth and men in white) are lined up on bamboo stretchers to await their turn. The main cremation site is the Manikarnika Ghat, revered because this was where Shiva, trying to retrieve an earring lost by his wife Parvati, dug out a basin which filled with his sweat. One end of this *ghat* bears the footprint of Vishnu, the preserver, and cremation here is reserved for important people.

The people of India have good cause to respect the Ganges, which flows for 2,500 km (1,550 miles) down from the central Himalayas to reach the plain in Uttar Pradesh, then across the Hindustan Plain to the Bay of Bengal. Though there are 38 longer rivers in the world, its importance to the country can hardly be over-estimated. Its enormous alluvial basin supports 300 million people and has nurtured a great civilization since earliest times. There are records of the use of the river water for irrigation as nearly as the 4th century BC, and the canal system was greatly extended by the Mogul emperors and later under British rule.

Though for much of its course the Ganges flows through India, most of the vast delta – the largest in the world – lies in Bangladesh. There the Ganges is joined by the Brahmaputra, which then forms countless channels as it flows to the sea. Though in West Bengal the channels are so full of silt that the water hardly flows, the delta rivers of Bangladesh are wide and fast and the monsoon rains regularly result in widespread floods. Such flooding adds greatly to the fertility of the flat land but, as there are no natural barriers to hold back the water, floods take a high toll in human life. In 1970 hurricane winds whipped up an enormous wave that devastated the densely populated, low-lying land. The official death toll was 300,000 but outside observers calculated that it was nearer 1 million. The people of the delta know both the blessings and the destructive power of 'Mother Ganga'.

INDEX

Page numbers in *italic* refer to the illustrations

PHOTOGRAPHIC
ACKNOWLEDGEMENTS

Bruce Coleman Limited: Jen and Des Bartlett 70-1, Nigel Blake 170-1, Jane Burton 112, Bob and Clara Calhoun 64-5, R. I. M. Campbell 18-19, Robert P. Carr 80-1, Alain Compost 184-5, Gerald Cubitt 22-3, 26-7, 160-1, David Davies 140-1, 141, Nicholas de Vore 65, 66-7, 123, 130-1, 132-3, Geoff Dore 142-3, Francisco J. Erize 90-1, J. Exelby 136-7, M. P. L. Fogden 2-3, Jeff Foott Productions 76-7, Michael Freeman 62-3, 74-5, Frances Furlong 122-3, 124-5, Francisco Futil 44-5, Keith Gunnar 94-5, Anthony Healy 111, Dr Charles Henneghien 28, 30-1, Dr M. P. Kahl 21, Steven C. Kaufman 52-3, Stephen J. Krasemann 50-1, Charlie Ott 78-9, Dieter and Mary Plage 9, 185, Dr Eckart Pott 24-5, Dr Sandro Prato 172-3, Michael P. Price 7 top, 38-9, 142, Norbert Rosing 72, 72-3, Dr Frieder Sauer 34-5, Norbert Schwirtz 148-9, John Shaw 77, 82, 82-3, Werner Stoy 6 bottom, 130, Sullivan and Rogers 96, Kim Taylor 118-19, Norman Tomalin 96-7, 129, Peter Ward 28-9, Paul R. Wilkinson 110-11, G. Ziesler 10-11; Susan Griggs Agency: Mike Andrews 48-9, George Hall 58-9; Highlands and Islands Enterprise 146-7; Hutchison Library 14-15, 40-1, 180-1: Timothy Beddow 12-13, Robert Francis 16-17, 138-9, 150-1, J. G. Fuller 46-7, P. Goycolea 100-1, Andrew Hill 34, Edward Parker 86-7, W. Von Puttkamar 88-9; A. F. Kersting 152-3; Mountain Camera: John Cleare 57, 60-1, 68-9, 69, 158-9, 164-5, Colin Monteath 102-3, 104-5, 106-7; Nature Photographers Ltd: Peter Davey 14, Roger Tidman 168, Derek Washington 36-7; New Zealand Tourism Office, London 126-7; Oxford Scientific Films: J. A. L. Cooke 80; Planet Earth Pictures: D. Barrett 92-3, John Lythgoe 120-1; Spectrum Colour Library 1, 42-3, 45, 56-7, 84-5, 112-13, 115, 162-3, 173, 176-7, 186-7; R. Gordon 114-15, Cris Haigh 7 bottom, 186, Dallas and John Heaton 5 bottom, 32-3, 51, J. Lochhead 151; Judy Todd 6 top, 87, 108-9, 134-5, 139, 144, 144-5, 182-3, 183; The Government of Western Australia 116-17; ZEFA 20-1, 41, 54-5, 154-5, 174-5: Dr Baer 188-9, B. Crader 128-9, Eckhard Gollnow 166-7, S. Sammer 178-9, I. Steinhoff 5 top, 33, H. Strass 98-9, C. Voight 156-7, M. Zur 168-9.